BIR~~~~ of

IT

POCKET PHOTO GUIDES

Marianne Taylor & Daniele Occhiato

H E L M

LONDON • OXFORD • NEW YORK • NEW DELHI • SYDNEY

HELM
Bloomsbury Publishing Plc
50 Bedford Square, London, WC1B 3DP, UK

BLOOMSBURY, HELM and the HELM logo are trademarks of
Bloomsbury Publishing Plc

First published in Great Britain, 2018

A catalogue record for this book is available from the British Library

Library of Congress Cataloguing-in-Publication data has been applied for

ISBN: TPB: 978-1-4729-4982-0; ePub: 978-1-4729-4983-7

2 4 6 8 10 9 7 5 3 1

Designed by Susan McIntyre
Printed and bound in China by RR Donnelley

To find out more about our authors and books visit www.bloomsbury.com
and sign up for our newsletters

CONTENTS

INTRODUCTION

Italy marks the transition from south-western to south-eastern Europe. The country comprises the mainland with its elegant high-heeled boot outline, which stretches south-east into the Mediterranean, along with the major islands of Sicily and Sardinia (plus a few groups of smaller islands). With its generally warm climate, varied and spectacular scenery, famous cityscapes and unique archaeological wonders, Italy is an extremely popular destination for tourists.

The history of Italy's wild places and wildlife has not been an entirely happy tale. Rapid industrialisation led to pollution, forest clearance, rapid development of formerly wild coastlines and the loss of vast tracts of habitats, while efforts to reduce the hunting of wild birds has met with strong resistance from a powerful gun lobby. However, much of Italy's wild beauty has survived intact, and conservation progress since the 1990s has been considerable. There are now 25 national parks in Italy and these, along with other protected areas, cover more than 11% of the total land area. One third of animal species native to Europe can be found in Italy, and about 540 bird species have been recorded here – well over half of all species recorded in Europe as a whole, although many of these are 'vagrants' rather than regular visitors. This book covers the most frequently encountered or distinctive birds of Italy – 256 species in all. For an exhaustive guide to all species ever observed in Italy, we recommend *Collins Bird Guide* (2009) – see Further reading on page 139.

HOW TO USE THIS BOOK

This pocket guide is designed to be a quick and easy reference book for anyone birdwatching in Italy. The introductory section presents general information, including types of habitat, some of the best birdwatching sites, and general guidance for birdwatching in the country. This is followed by accounts for individual species, arranged by family. A glossary covering basic terminology is included towards the back of the book.

Each account is illustrated with one or more colour photographs, showing the bird as it will be encountered in Italy – so winter visitors are shown in winter plumage, summer visitors in breeding plumage, and where the sexes differ significantly, male and female plumages are shown. The images show wild birds photographed in Italy, and are chosen to show a clear view in natural viewing conditions, with good natural light.

The text describes the bird's appearance in all plumages likely to be seen in Italy, highlighting key features that will particularly aid identification. Songs and calls are then described, followed by information on the bird's habitat preference in Italy, any notable behavioural details, and finally an outline of its distribution, abundance and seasons of occurrence. For those species assigned a conservation status of Near Threatened or Vulnerable by the International Union for Conservation of Nature (IUCN), this is mentioned in brackets at the start of the account. A few technical terms are used to save space but all are explained fully in the glossary.

BIRD TOPOGRAPHY

The illustration below shows a quick guide to body parts and feather groups referred to in the species accounts. An understanding of these terms will be useful for identification purposes.

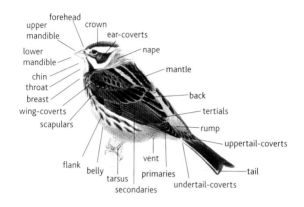

HABITATS

Italy's shape and location gives it considerable variation in climate from north to south. The land profile also varies a great deal – much of the mainland is hilly or mountainous but there are also some important lowland wetlands, and more than 9,000km of coastline. The two major islands, Sicily and Sardinia, have their own particular geographic character and wildlife.

Mountains Italy's northern edge is marked by the Alps, Europe's highest and most significant mountain range. A few cold-climate montane species, such as Ptarmigan, occur only here, while other mountain-dwelling birds can also be found in the Apennines further south, in the uplands of the south, and on Sicily and Sardinia.

Forest There are significant remnants of primeval deciduous forest in Calabria and Tuscany, while in the alpine regions there are forests of fir and pine, home to Capercaillies, Nutcrackers and many more birds. The Apennine foothills support interesting woodlands of Neapolitan maple and Italian alder. On Sicily, Sardinia and the southern mainland, woodland is dominated by Mediterranean species such as cork oak and Aleppo pine.

Scrub/maquis Where forest has been cleared, or the soil does not support its growth, a mosaic of bushes and tall herbaceous plants may grow. This is rich in insect life and accordingly supports a great range of bird species, including various species of shrikes and *Sylvia* warblers. Maquis scrub, consisting mainly of thick evergreen shrubs like broom and myrtle, is common in the south and on Sicily and Sardinia.

Meadows and cultivated land Untouched grassland is scarce in Italy but alpine meadows offer great hunting grounds for birds and other wildlife, especially butterflies. Vineyards, olive groves, grazing land and other farmland can also be productive for open-country and scrubland birds.

Rivers and lakes Italy has few major rivers, the longest being the 650-km long Po, with its source in the western Alps. Upland rivers and streams support their own specialist birds, such as Dippers, while lowland rivers attract a variety of wetland species, and European Bee-eaters, Kingfishers and Sand Martins nest in river banks. The high, steep-banked glacial lakes support rather few birds, but well-vegetated lowland lakes attract many species.

Marshland The most important area of marshland in Italy is the Po Delta in the north-east, but smaller marshes, lagoons and wetlands can be found elsewhere, for example the Circeo National Park on the Lazio coast. They support many breeding birds and offer rest and respite for migrant waders and wildfowl.

Coasts, islands and offshore Much of the Italian coastline has been developed for tourism, but there remain some unspoilt stretches of rocky shoreline and extensive sand dunes. Tiny rocky islets provide breeding sites for special birdlife including Eleonora's Falcon and Scopoli's Shearwater, while some seabirds winter offshore around the Mediterranean Sea and may be observed from headlands.

Urban environments Town parks and gardens often support more common woodland birds, and colonies of exotic feral birds like Rose-ringed Parakeets. Archaeological sites and older settlements can be wonderful places to seek out birdlife – for example, the beautiful walled city of Matera in Basilicata, with its famous Lesser Kestrel colony.

BIRDWATCHING IN ITALY

Italy has many national parks, nature reserves and other protected areas, and also a number of long-distance hiking trails that traverse some of the most spectacularly scenic parts of the country. In the countryside in general, you'll find many paths and tracks with open access, and locals will usually be happy to offer advice if needed. In short, exploring wild places in Italy is very safe and straightforward, although venturing onto the more challenging alpine and other mountain trails will require a good level of fitness, as well as careful preparation and common sense. Take the usual precautions when out for a walk – carry water, sun protection and a charged mobile phone.

Walking maps from Tabacco Casa Editrice cover many areas, and there are many English-language regional walking guides available, with recommended routes mapped and described in detail. Some national parks also sell their own maps and guides. Nature reserves and national parks will usually have waymarked trails for you to follow, and some have hides for closer views of key spots. You will need binoculars, and a telescope will be useful, particularly at the coast and in the mountains.

Hunting is widespread in Italy, and the hunting season is long, beginning on the first Sunday in September and continuing through to the end of February or March depending on the quarry species (until the end of January for birds). It is prohibited in some but not all protected wild places – be wary of leaving main hiking routes during the open season, and some sites are best avoided altogether at this time as they will simply not offer productive birding. Illegal killing of protected species, particularly raptors, is still a frequent problem. If you see anything that raises concerns, contact LIPU (BirdLife in Italy, www.lipu.it) for advice. As in other countries with a long hunting tradition, you may find that birds are very wary of humans and close approach may be difficult, although this will vary from region to region (and some species seem naturally fearless anyway).

Many birding tour companies offer trips to Italy, particularly to regions such as the Po Delta, Alps and Sicily. This is the easiest way for a newcomer to Italian birding to connect with the more unusual species, while more general-interest tours will usually also offer some birding opportunities. Independent travellers may wish to contact a local birder for a more informal arrangement – try the Birding Pals website: www.birdingpal.org/Italy.htm.

LOCALITIES

The map on page 9 shows some of the best and most accessible birding sites in Italy. There are, of course, many more for the adventurous traveller to discover. Explore information on protected sites in Italy here: www.parks.it/Eindex.php.

1. Parco Nazionale dello Stelvio (Lombardy) An expanse of alpine mountains with more than 1,500km of paths; borders several other national parks. Montane and forest birds, including Golden Eagle, Eagle Owl and five woodpecker species.

2. Parco Nazionale Gran Paradiso (Piedmont) This vast national park holds the full suite of alpine habitat types and associated birdlife.

3. Riserva Naturale della Foce dell'Isonzo (Friuli Venezia Giulia) Situated in the eastern part of the Po Delta, this wetland nature reserve has superb viewing facilities and attracts large numbers of waders, wildfowl and herons.

4. Parco Naturale del Delta del Po (Emilia-Romagna) An extensive, spectacular area of marshland and open water, home to Gull-billed Tern, Ferruginous Duck and many more wetland birds.

5. Parco Nazionale Dolomiti Bellunesi (Veneto) A very large and diverse protected area in the Dolomites, good for montane species such as Rock Partridge.

6. Riserva Naturale Integrale Lastoni Selva Pezzi (Veneto) Upland forest and mountain, notable for raptors, owls and woodpeckers.

7. Parco di Migliarino San Rossore, Massaciuccoli (Tuscany) This Tuscan natural park is a rare area of unspoilt coastline, comprising beach, lake, scrubland and forest, and is a key migration stopover as well as hosting numerous wintering and breeding birds. LIPU protects Lake Massaciuccoli as a bird reserve and offers guided boat trips.

8. Padule di Fucecchio (Tuscany) Italy's largest inland wetland. A nature reserve with several hides; holds a very large mixed heronry (up to 1,300 pairs of Night Heron, Little Egret, Squacco Heron, Cattle Egret, Grey Heron, Great Egret and Purple Heron).

9. Capraia (Tuscany) A remote and beautiful island, part of the protected Arcipelago Toscano, with nesting Cory's Shearwater and Marmora's Warbler.

10. Parco Nazionale del Gran Sasso e Monti della Laga (Lazio/Abruzzo) In the heart of the Apennines, this is one of Italy's largest national parks, with exceptional botanical biodiversity, and birdlife including Golden Eagle, Wallcreeper and White-winged Snowfinch.

11. Parco Nazionale del Circeo (Lazio) Formed of a great crescent-shaped dune, ancient coastal forest and a series of lakes surrounded by marshland, this very picturesque national park supports a great range of birdlife.

12. Parco Nazionale Alta Murgia (Apulia) With its wild open plains, this national park offers a kind of scenery that is scarce in Italy. A key area for Lesser Kestrel, also steppe birds like Black-eared Wheatear and Calandra Lark.

13. Riserva Statale Torre Guaceto (Apulia) A large and important area of Mediterranean maquis scrub; habitat for shrikes, warblers and other scrubland species.

14. Stretto di Messina (Calabria/Sicily) Italy forms a flyway for large, soaring migratory birds that prefer to avoid sea crossings, and many cross from the mainland to Sicily via the narrow Strait of Messina, offering exciting spring and autumn birdwatching.

15. Riserva Naturale Orientata Zingaro (Sicily) A diverse and beautiful stretch of coastline, which is good for watching seabirds and finding scrubland species.

16. Parco Naturale Regionale Molentargius (Sardinia) Extensive lagoons and marshland, with breeding Greater Flamingo and many other wetland birds.

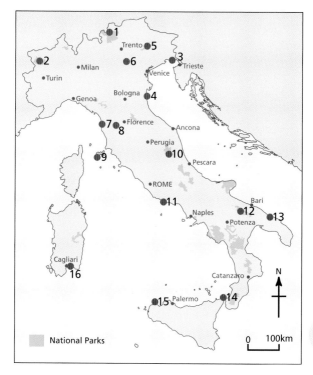

SEASONS

The following terms are used to describe periods of occurrence in Italy for the birds in this book.

Resident Species that can be found all year round. Note, though, that the same species may be resident in some parts of the country but occur only as a visitor in others. For many resident species, the population increases considerably in winter as more birds arrive from northern and eastern Europe.

Summer visitor Species that visit for the breeding season only, migrating south in winter. Present from spring until autumn.

Winter visitor Species that visit for winter only, and migrate north to breed. Present from autumn until spring.

Passage migrant Species that neither breed nor winter in Italy, but pass through on their migratory journey, so can usually be seen in spring and again in autumn. Some passage migrants also overwinter or oversummer, but in much smaller numbers.

GREYLAG GOOSE *Anser anser* 80cm

A large, robust goose with rather uniform grey-brown plumage at rest, marked with narrow pale bars on upperparts and dark barring on flanks. Undertail is white. In flight shows contrasting light blue-grey forewings, pale grey-brown rump, and grey-brown tail with white at base and tip. Eyes dark, prominent in pale head. Bill large, orange with whitish tip. Legs pale dull pink. Gives loud honking and cackling calls, like farmyard goose (domesticated Greylag). A passage migrant and winter visitor to lowland wetlands and fields, with small breeding populations in the north-east. Feral domestic Greylags are usually plumper than wild birds, and often partially or wholly white.

RED-BREASTED MERGANSER *Mergus serrator* 55cm

A large, slender, fish-eating diving duck. Male has dark green-glossed head, white neck-ring, reddish lower neck and breast, black-and-white upperparts and grey underparts. Female and eclipse male drabber with reddish-brown head. Both sexes have shaggy crests and show much white in the wing in flight (particularly the male). Eyes red or brownish-red. Bill red, long, narrow with hooked tip and serrated cutting edges for catching fish. Call a low, grating *kraak kraak*. Sits low in the water and makes frequent lengthy dives. Most likely to be seen offshore on sheltered coasts, sometimes in groups. Passage migrant and winter visitor; some birds stay through summer.

▼ *Adult female*

▼ *Adult male*

SHELDUCK *Tadorna tadorna* 60cm

A large, striking duck of mainly coastal habitats. Mostly white with head glossed blackish-green, broad red-brown breast-band, black line down belly centre, black shoulder-stripes, flight-feathers and tail-tip, pale orange undertail. Eyes dark, legs pink, bill pinkish-red (with prominent knob at base in male). Juvenile mostly white with no breast-band, greyish head and upperparts, pink bill. Vocal, especially when breeding, with various whistling and honking calls. A gregarious duck of flat muddy shorelines and saltmarsh, also sometimes inland on lake shores and grassy fields. Resident in parts of north-east and north-west Italy, Sicily and Sardinia, more widespread in winter.

POCHARD *Aythya ferina* 45cm

(Vulnerable) A compact diving duck with peaked crown and sloping forehead. Male has dark coppery-red head, red eyes, black breast, rump, undertail and tail, and light silvery-grey wings, back and underparts. Female light grey-brown with dark eyes, diffuse broad barring on flanks and back, faint pale 'spectacles' and pale area near bill base, but rather variable. Bill dark with wide, pale grey band. Female gives loud purring call in flight. Dives often, also feeds at the surface. Breeds on lakes and marshland with some deeper water (more than 1 metre deep) and lush marginal vegetation for nesting; in winter on all kinds of open waters. Localised resident, widespread and locally abundant in winter.

▽ *Adult male*

▽ *Adult female*

▲ Adult male ▲ Adult female (front)

FERRUGINOUS DUCK *Aythya nyroca* **40cm**

(Near Threatened) Small, dark-looking diving duck with distinctly peaked head shape. Male dark reddish-brown with clear-cut white undertail and white eyes. Female similar but with less of a reddish tint, eyes dark. In flight shows wide white wing-bar and white belly. Bill grey in both sexes with black tip and faintly paler band near tip. Note that some female Tufted Ducks show a white undertail – check head shape, eye colour and body plumage colour. Female gives a purring flight call; male whistles and clucks in courtship. A shy breeding bird of lush marshy lakes. Very localised but more widespread on migration.

TUFTED DUCK *Aythya fuligula* **44cm**

A smallish diving duck, with long dangling crest at back of head. Male glossy black with white flanks, female warm dark brown with paler flanks. Some females have white 'blaze' around bill base and/or white undertail. Both sexes have yellow eyes and show white belly in flight. Juvenile has duller eyes and shorter tuft than adult. Bill grey with broad black tip and suggestion of paler band near tip. Female has growling call, courting male a fast turkey-like chatter. Dives for food; prefers lakes with some deep water. Localised resident but widespread winter visitor.

GARGANEY *Spatula querquedula* 39cm

Small, slim and elegant, longish-billed dabbling duck. Male has dark brown head with very conspicuous broad white supercilium, brown neck and breast, grey body with elongated, dark-edged scapulars, spotted tail and undertail. In flight shows light blue forewing. Female mid-brown with darker mottling, well-marked face with dark stripes through and below the eye, pale spot near bill base. Male gives dry rattling call in courtship, female quiet but may give soft quack or cackle. Nests discreetly in undisturbed marshy areas and visits shallow, well-vegetated lakes on migration. A summer visitor, scarce in the south; common and widespread passage migrant.

▲ *Adult male* ▼ *Adult female*

SHOVELER *Spatula clypeata* 48cm

A medium-large, short-necked dabbling duck. Easily identified in all plumages by its very long broad bill, usually held tilted downwards. Male has dark green-glossed head, white breast and rear flanks, and chestnut flanks and belly; shows light blue forewings in flight. Female is brown with darker streaking and mottling; in flight shows pale grey forewings and all-brown belly with contrasting whitish underwings. Calls are hoarse quacks and wheezes. Feeds mainly on surface, with characteristic very flat-backed stance, using its large bill to filter out food items. Visits shallow open waters and marshlands. Common. Widespread passage migrant and winter visitor; scarce and localised breeder.

▲ *Adult male* ▼ *Adult female*

▲ Adult male ▲ Adult female

GADWALL *Mareca strepera* 51cm

Slightly smaller and more delicately built than Mallard. A rather drab dabbling duck – male mostly light speckled grey with jet-black undertail and rump, chestnut patch in wing (often hidden), dark eyes and dark grey bill. Female mottled brown with dark eye-stripe, white belly and white underwing, dark bill with light orange sides. Both sexes have white speculum, obvious in flight but sometimes hidden when bird is resting on water. Legs and feet light orange-yellow. Female has Mallard-like quack, male a soft whistle and harsh croak. Mainly found on well-vegetated lakes. Widespread passage migrant and winter visitor, scarce and localised breeding bird.

WIGEON *Mareca penelope* 46cm

Attractive, compact dabbling duck with rounded head and small, neat bill. Male has reddish head with cream-yellow crown-stripe, pink breast, grey body with white rear flanks and black tail. Shows large white oval on wing in flight. Female warm red-brown, with white belly and diffuse darkish eye-mask. Both sexes have dark eyes, and light grey bill with black tip. Male has loud *whee-ooo* whistle, female a growling note. Spends more time out of water than most ducks, grazing on fields near water, often in very large flocks, sometimes alongside flocks of geese. Also visits lakes and marshland. Widespread and locally abundant winter visitor and passage migrant.

▲ From left: adult male, adult female

▲ Adult male

MALLARD *Anas platyrhynchos* 55cm

Large, familiar dabbling duck. Male has yellow bill, bottle-green head, narrow white neck-ring, chestnut breast, grey body with black stern (two central feathers tightly up-curled). Female mottled brown, paler on belly, dark eye-stripe, bill brown with variable orange patches. Both sexes have dark eyes and iridescent deep blue speculum. Female gives loud quack, male soft clucking note. Found on all kinds of fresh water, including lakes in town parks. Resident and common throughout Italy. Domestic Mallards may be seen in the wild – they come in a confusing range of colours and body shapes but males always show the characteristic curled tail feathers.

PINTAIL *Anas acuta* 55cm (+10cm tail in male)

A slender, elegant dabbling duck. Looks very elongated and slim in flight. Male has dark brown head and neck, white breast extending in narrow white line up neck-sides, grey body, white belly, elongated black central tail-feathers. Female plain brown, best told by unmarked face and slim, long-tailed build, showing narrow whitish wing-bar and white trailing edge to wing in flight.

▲ Adult male ▼ Adult female

Both sexes have dark eyes, grey bill and legs. Male's call a soft purring whistle, female's a cawing quack. Found on lakes and marshes with some open water. Widespread winter visitor and passage migrant in Italy.

▲ Adult male breeding

▲ Adult female

EURASIAN TEAL *Anas crecca* 36cm

The smallest dabbling duck. Compact, short-necked and relatively small-billed. Male has chestnut head with broad green stripe from eye to nape, edged finely in yellow. Breast buff with dark speckles, undertail yellow with black border. Shows broad white wing-bar in flight. Female is rather plain brown, belly pale, wing-bar narrower. Both sexes have green speculum. Flight fast and wader-like. Male's call a short, high-pitched purring *prroop*, female's a quiet quack. Shy, often reluctant to venture into open water; often feeds on muddy or vegetated shorelines of lakes, and also visits marshland. A localised breeder but common and widespread winter visitor.

COMMON QUAIL *Coturnix coturnix* 17cm

The smallest gamebird. Plump, short-necked and short-tailed, but with proportionately long wings and fast, strong flight. Plumage light grey-brown, marked with broad pale and dark streaks, most prominently on flanks. Has pale supercilium and crown-stripe; male has black centre to throat. Very shy and difficult to see, most often detected by male's song. This is given most persistently at dawn and dusk and is a repeated, rhythmic three-note whistle with longer space between notes 1 and 2 than between 2 and 3, sometimes rendered as *wet… my-lips*. Breeds in open, well-vegetated lowlands, including lush grassland and fields of dense crops. A widespread summer visitor.

ROCK PARTRIDGE   *Alectoris graeca*   34cm

(Near Threatened) A stout, relatively large partridge with colourful markings. Body blue-grey, shading to brown on back and yellowish-brown on belly. Flanks boldly marked with broad black-and-white bars. Chin and throat white with clear-cut broad black border – although in the Sicilian subspecies (*whitakeri*) this black ring is often very narrow or broken at throat. Bill, legs and eye-ring scarlet. The territorial call is uneven, quite rapid series of hoarse notes. Favours rocky and mountainous habitats with some vegetation, mainly 1,000–2,000 metres (but avoids north-facing slopes). Gregarious and sometimes conspicuous – will perch on prominent rocks. Resident on high Alps, Apennines and southern mountains.

BARBARY PARTRIDGE   *Alectoris barbara*   33cm

Resembles Red-legged Partridge but has grey rather than white chin and supercilium, giving plainer appearance. Body plumage grey-brown with boldly barred flanks, orange-brown belly and undertail, broad blackish crown-stripe, reddish eye-stripe, grey chin and throat bordered with streaky dark reddish 'neck-shawl'. Bill and legs red. Call a series of short notes with fast, regular rhythm, also raucous three-note call like that of Red-legged Partridge. Found in a variety of habitats, especially more open and rocky terrain. Resident and fairly common on Sardinia – one of only a handful of European populations of this primarily North African species.

RED-LEGGED PARTRIDGE *Alectoris rufa* 33cm

Very like Rock Partridge, but has smaller white chin patch, and black collar extends onto greyish neck as streaky dark 'neck-shawl'. Also has white supercilium, less bold flank streaks (black and light grey rather than black and white). Like other partridges is reluctant to fly, preferring to escape danger on foot. Flies fast with shallow wingbeats, and in flight shows dark red-brown tail-sides, contrasting with blue-grey of lower back and rump. Most familiar call is harsh three-note *kuh chuh-chuh* but will give notes in longer series at times. Lives in rocky terrain, farmland, field edges; only in north-west Italy.

COMMON PHEASANT *Phasianus colchicus* 60–80cm (male larger)

A well known gamebird. Adult males are unmistakeable, with dark green head ornamented with ear-tufts and scarlet facial wattles. Some have white neck-ring. Body plumage rich reds, blue-greys and browns with dark and white markings, tail very long with dark barring. Female plain mottled brown with long tail, but short-tailed young birds could be confused with other gamebirds. Melanistic and leucistic (white) forms may occur. Call a loud crowing two-note cluck; male's song a longer series, accompanied with noisy wing-fluttering. All kinds of countryside habitats with good ground cover. Introduced to Italy for shooting; common widespread resident.

▲ Adult female   ▲ Adult male

HAZEL GROUSE *Tetrastes bonasia* 37cm

A small, long-tailed grouse with short peaked crest (sometimes held flatter). Plumage finely and intricately marked with brown, grey and black streaks, scalloping and mottling; has blackish tail-tip, unmarked grey rump, and white 'shoulder straps'. Male has black throat, female's throat speckled grey and white. Shy and keeps in cover, relying on camouflage, but takes flight through the trees as soon as it is startled. Has short, fluting alarm call and male's song is series of thin, trilling, high-pitched notes, recalling much smaller bird. Found in dense pine and birch forest. Alpine regions, resident.

PTARMIGAN *Lagopus muta* 33cm

Elegant, smallish grouse, adapted to endure harsh, cold climates and prolonged annual snow cover. In summer, grey-brown above with white wings, belly and (fully feathered) legs – male has black lores and red 'combs' above eyes. Through autumn, plumage transitions to entirely white, except for tail, which remains black in all plumages. During moult, upperside plumage patched with white. Has various dry snorting or snoring calls. Gregarious, especially in winter and sometimes very confiding, moving slowly across rocky ground in search of food. Fast direct flight. A bird of high snowy mountains, found only in Alps in Italy.

▲ *Adult male*   ▲ *Adult female*

CAPERCAILLIE *Tetrao urogallus* 60–88cm (male much larger)

A very large, imposing grouse, recalling turkey in build, with long, heavy tail. Male blackish, shading to dark brown on back, with some paler markings on flanks, undertail and tail. Small red wattle above eye. Bill strong, hooked, pale horn in colour. Female smaller but still a substantial bird; finely patterned in grey-brown and black, with rusty tinge on breast and throat, bill dark. Shy and quick to flush, often perching in trees. Quiet except when displaying at communal leks, when males strut with fanned tails, giving loud croaks and grunts. Resident in mature pine forest in Alpine regions.

BLACK GROUSE *Lyrurus tetrix* 40–58cm

Smaller, more elegant and smaller-headed than Capercaillie. Male ('blackcock') black with white undertail and wing-bar. Long lyre-shaped tail, prominent red wattle over eye, bill small and dark. Female ('greyhen') smaller, with shorter blunt-ended tail, finely patterned with dark and pale barring and mottling on grey-brown background. Differs from much larger female Capercaillie in lacking reddish tint on breast; also shows narrow white wing-bar in flight. Males display communally at leks, leaping, fighting and posturing, flaring white undertails, giving cackling and bubbling calls. Pine and birch forest, moorland, clearings, heaths and boggy ground with open water. Resident in Alps.

▼ *Adult male*   ▼ *Adult female*

GREATER FLAMINGO *Phoenicopterus roseus* 133cm

Unmistakeable. Tall with very long legs and very long slender neck. Large, deep-based, steeply down-curved bill. At rest looks mainly whitish-pink, with legs and bill darker, bill tipped black, neck held in graceful 'S' curve. In flight holds neck and legs fully outstretched; reveals black flight feathers and bright pinkish-red underwings and forewings. Juvenile drab grey-brown with dark legs, gradually whitening with maturity. Gives goose-like cackles in flight. Feeding flocks move together in close proximity, heads lowered upside-down into water, keeping up constant low-pitched murmur. Found at shallow lagoons, sea bays and salt lakes. Gregarious but localised colonial breeder; more widespread in winter and on migration.

LITTLE GREBE *Tachybaptus ruficollis* 26cm

A very small, compact water bird, seldom seen on land or in flight. Short pointed bill. Looks tail-less on water, with fluffy-looking rear end. Breeding plumage blackish, shading to dark chestnut on cheeks, neck and flanks, whitish at rear of body, with prominent circle of bare yellow skin around gape. Bill and eyes dark. Juvenile and non-breeding plumage paler, with brown upperparts and warm buff underparts, bill paler, gape marking less prominent. Chick grey with black-and-white head-stripes, traces of which still show in juvenile plumage. Gives loud whinnying chatter when breeding. Dives frequently when feeding. All inland waters; common, widespread resident.

△ *Adult breeding*
▽ *Adult non-breeding*

▲ Adult winter
◀ Adult summer

GREAT CRESTED GREBE *Podiceps cristatus* 49cm

Slender, elegant water bird. Upperparts brown, flanks lighter buff-grey. Face, throat, breast and belly white, lores dark. In breeding plumage has long dark ear-tufts and chestnut, black-edged facial ruff, dark bill, dark red eyes. In winter lacks ruff and tufts, bill becomes pink. Looks white when rolling over to preen belly. Chick striped black and white all over; juvenile shows traces of stripes on face until early winter. Noisy croaks and rattling calls in breeding season, especially during elaborate courtship display. Dives often, catches sizeable fish. Nests on inland waters; in winter also forms large rafts at sea in sheltered waters. A common, widespread resident.

BLACK-NECKED GREBE *Podiceps nigricollis* 31cm

▲ Adult summer ▼ Adult winter

A small, dainty grebe. Markedly peaked crown, fine pointed bill with slight upward tilt. In breeding plumage dark but colourful, with black head, neck and breast, reddish flanks, and tuft of yellow feathers flaring out behind bright red eye. In winter looks monochrome, blackish-grey above, paler below, with dusky collar and whitish rear end. Red eye prominent. Chick grey with black-and-white striped head, juvenile like adult winter but with duller eye, pale orange wash on breast and cheek-sides. Gives *pu-iih* call on breeding grounds. Breeds in loose colonies on well-vegetated inland waters. Winters in estuaries, bays and lakes. Localised and irregular breeding bird; widespread in winter.

WOODPIGEON *Columba palumbus* 40cm

Large, plump, small-headed pigeon. Mainly light grey, shading to pink on breast and browner on wings. White neck patch and wing edge. In flight shows broad white wing-band, dark flight-feathers and tail-band. Eye whitish, bill yellow with pink base, legs pink. Juvenile lacks white neck patch, has darker eyes and bill. Feeds on ground and in trees, often loudly claps wings when taking flight. In breeding season performs display flight with wing-clapping ascent, gliding descent. Song a loud five-note *coo*. Found in woodland, parks, gardens and farmland. Gregarious in winter, may make cold-weather movements in very large flocks. Common and widespread resident, locally abundant in winter and on migration.

TURTLE DOVE *Streptopelia turtur* 26cm

(Vulnerable) Smallish, long-tailed, colourful dove. Head grey, shading to pinkish-grey on breast. Black-and-white striped patch on neck. Back and wing feathers dark with bright orange-brown fringes, giving 'tortoiseshell' pattern. In flight shows distinctive tail pattern – underside white with broad black base, upperparts dark with white edges; underwings grey. Bill small and slim, prominent red eye-ring, legs reddish. Juvenile patterned like adult but paler and drabber, lacks striped neck patch. Song a soft, soothing purr or croon, often given from overhead wire or other prominent perch. Favours woodland and farmland with scattered trees and copses. A common but declining summer visitor and passage migrant.

COLLARED DOVE *Streptopelia decaocto* 31cm
. . . .
Larger and much paler and plainer than Turtle Dove. Plumage light pinkish-fawn with narrow, white-edged, black half-collar on neck (absent in juvenile). In flight shows dark wingtips, pale greyish band across forewings, pale tail-sides, undertail pure white with dark at base only. Eyes dark reddish without obvious eye-ring, bill small and dark, legs pink. Song recalls Woodpigeon but has more strained sound, and comprises three notes, stress on middle note, can recall Cuckoo's song. Gregarious in winter, can be very confiding. Lowlands where food supplies are abundant, especially on farmland and around settlements. A common resident.

EUROPEAN NIGHTJAR *Caprimulgus europaeus* 26cm
. . . .
A nocturnal bird with distinctive long-tailed, long-winged, falcon-like shape, and superbly camouflaged plumage. Intricately mottled, speckled and barred in shades of grey and brown, with whitish 'tramlines' on back and pale markings on cheeks and chin-sides. Male in flight shows white tail-corners and white patches near wingtips. Rests by day on ground or perching along branch, relying on camouflage. At night, hawks for moths and other insects in agile, silent flight. Male sings from dusk, a continuous soft purring *churr*, recalling radio interference; also wing-clapping display flight. Breeds on heathland and moors, and in bogs and forest clearings. Widespread summer visitor.

ALPINE SWIFT *Tachymarptis melba* 21cm

Largest swift; sturdy and powerful in flight. Wings long, sickle-shaped, tail forked. Upperparts dull mid-brown, underparts similar but with clean-cut white throat patch and belly patch – throat patch hard to see at distance. Flies with slower, less flickering wingbeats than smaller swift species. Loud, long, rapid twittering call, falling in pace and pitch. Flies in groups around breeding grounds and may forage long distances from nest, catching insects in flight and (when feeding young) collecting bolus of food in throat pouch, forming obvious swelling to chin. Nests in rocky crevices and buildings in highlands and lowlands. A scarce but widespread summer visitor and passage migrant.

PALLID SWIFT *Apus pallidus* 17cm

Dark brown swift with large, diffuse pale throat patch, dark 'mask' around eyes, and distinct paler fringing to body feathers, giving scaly appearance. However, difficult to separate from Common Swift without well-lit, good views. Slightly broader-winged with slower flight than Common Swift, with lower-pitched screaming call; wings show more contrast between dark coverts and paler secondaries; when seen from above shows contrast between dark rump and pale inner secondaries. Nests in crevices on buildings, most common near coast. Highly aerial and gregarious. A summer visitor, much less abundant than Common Swift but may be seen in the same areas.

COMMON SWIFT *Apus apus* 17cm

A blackish-brown, uniform swift with small, usually quite indistinct paler throat patch. Shows little contrast otherwise, though juvenile slightly paler overall with Pallid-like scaly appearance to body. Agile aerial hunter of insects, trapping them in wide mouth fringed with stiff hair-like feathers. Has fast flickering flight with rapid twists and turns. Flies high in fine weather but in bad weather will skim ground. Call a thin drawn-out scream, given in unison by groups flying around their nest-sites (with birds in nests answering in kind). Nests mainly in crevices in buildings and hunts over open country, wetlands and urban environments. Very common, widespread summer visitor.

COMMON CUCKOO *Cuculus canorus* 34cm

A hawk-like bird with long tail and long pointed wings, short yellow legs. Distinctive perched posture with wings drooped. Upperparts grey (tinted brown in female), belly white with fine black bars; female also occurs in rare rufous ('hepatic') morph. Juvenile browner, barred all over. Bill small, slightly down-curved. Has yellow eye-ring, light brown eye. Male's song is two-note hollow *cuk-oo*, female has a fast mellow bubbling trill. A brood parasite of small birds such as Robins and Reed Warblers. Cuckoo chick ejects host's eggs/chicks and is reared alone by host parents. Common summer visitor, adults departing in early summer, juveniles in autumn.

WATER RAIL *Rallus aquaticus* 24cm

A shy bird of well-vegetated wetlands. Warm brown above with black streaks, plain lead-grey face and underparts, with fine black-and-white barring on flanks. Stout build with longish neck, long red bill, short pointed tail often cocked to reveal white underside, round-winged in flight. Legs pink, longish with very long slim toes. Juvenile paler and browner with yellowish bill and legs, lacks lead-grey tones, pale face with darkish eye-stripe. Has loud squealing piglet-like call. Forages discreetly in reeds and sedges at water's edge, and sometimes swims. May forage more in open in winter. Lowland lakes and marshland. A widespread resident.

SPOTTED CRAKE *Porzana porzana* 21cm

A very shy bird of rough wet grassland. A little smaller than Water Rail, longer-winged, with a much shorter, thick-based bill. Plumage basically grey on underparts, brown on upperparts, heavily marked with white spotting below (becoming barring on flanks), and black spots above. Front of face blackish, undertail unmarked whitish-buff. Bill reddish, legs dull green. Juvenile paler, with duller bill. Male's territorial 'song' a distinctive upslurred whistle, recalling whip-crack, most often heard at night. Stays in cover, slips out of view when disturbed, reluctant to fly. Lowland lakes and marshland. Widespread on migration, rare and very localised breeder.

▲ *Adult male*

▲ *Adult female*

LITTLE CRAKE *Zapornia parva* 18cm

A small, long-legged crake. Male patterned like Water Rail with grey face and underparts, brown upperparts but with plain grey, unbarred flanks and barred undertail. Female has grey only on face, underparts otherwise pale buff; juvenile similar but with brown-barred flanks. Bill small, yellow with red base. Legs greenish. Male's song, given at night, a short barking *kua* repeated in accelerating series. Inhabits reedbeds with bulrushes in marshy areas with some deeper water. Shy, mainly keeping to cover, but sometimes swims; climbs easily in low reed stems. Scarce summer visitor to northern Italy, and widespread passage migrant.

MOORHEN *Gallinula chloropus* 29cm

Familiar, conspicuous water bird. Plumage blackish, grey-tinted on underparts, brownish on wings. Has white undertail, and line of white streaks on flank form a broken stripe. Red frontal shield, bill red with yellow tip. Legs dull green. Juvenile dull grey-brown, paler on underparts, bill dull, no frontal shield, but does have adult's white side-stripe and undertail. Very vocal, with various short sneezing notes and longer liquid calls. Swims in pert stance with tail raised, constantly bobbing head, feeds at surface (does not dive). Flicks tail constantly when walking on land. Readily climbs and perches in trees. Found in all kinds of well-vegetated wetlands. Common resident.

COOT *Fulica atra* 39cm

Stout, almost tail-less water bird, smaller than most ducks. Adult plumage entirely sooty grey-black, darkest on head. Shows narrow white trailing edge to wing in flight. Eye dark red, bill and frontal shield white. Legs grey, toes have fleshy lobes. Juvenile greyer, whitish on underparts. Downy chick black with bald crown and prominent orange filoplumes on head (which otherwise similar Moorhen chick lacks). Dives for food, less comfortable on land than Moorhen but will eat grass on lake shores. Gregarious and vocal; gives various croaks and sharp calls. Found on reservoirs, lakes and slow large rivers, also town park ponds. A common resident.

COMMON CRANE *Grus grus* 110cm

Very large, stately bird, with long legs and neck, elongated tertial feathers creating appearance of large shaggy 'tail' when perched. Plumage grey, back mottled with brown in breeding season. Rear of neck white, throat and crown black with small red central crown patch. Eye red, shortish bill horn-coloured, legs grey. Juvenile has plain buffish head and lacks shaggy rear end. Flies with neck and legs outstretched, shows black flight feathers – small white 'landing light' marking at wing-bend. Loud bugling call in flight. A scarce and local winter visitor but common passage migrant, most often seen flying in long skeins; flocks also feed on fields.

RED-THROATED DIVER *Gavia stellata* **61cm**

The smallest diver, with distinctive slim slightly up-tilted bill. Breeding plumage (uncommon in Italy) brownish above with smooth blue-grey head and neck, red throat patch, fine white stripes on back of neck. Bill dark, eye red. In winter plumage looks grey above, white below, and on neck-sides when seen from behind. Eye usually prominent on white cheek. Upperside finely white-speckled. Shows white belly when performing rolling preen. In flight looks very elongated, feet projecting well beyond body, with slight 'sag' to outstretched neck. Silent in winter. Comfortable on water, rarely comes to land in winter. Makes lengthy and frequent dives to find prey. Winter visitor to sheltered northern seas.

BLACK-THROATED DIVER *Gavia arctica* **69cm**

Larger and more robust than Red-throated Diver, with heavier, straighter bill. Breeding plumage (uncommon in Italy) dark grey above with large white spots on back, smooth blue-grey head and neck, black throat patch, fine white stripes on sides of neck and breast. Winter plumage dull dark grey above, white below, shows no white neck-sides from behind, and grey on crown extends further down cheek, making eye less prominent. Similar cigar-shaped flight outline to Red-throated, but flight heavier, projecting feet and drooping neck even more noticeable. Silent in winter. A winter visitor to sheltered bays and estuaries around most of the coastline, also further offshore.

SCOPOLI'S SHEARWATER *Calonectris diomedea* 48cm

Fairly large seabird with large head, very long wings, larger and paler than Yelkouan Shearwater. Upperparts pale grey-brown with lighter feather fringes on back giving scaly impression. Flight feathers darker. Throat and belly white, underwings white with dark edging. Tail short, wedge-shaped, with narrow white rump patch. Bill stout, yellow with dark band. Flies gracefully with glides and relaxed flapping, skimming waves. Also swims, looking buoyant and gull-like on water. Often forages and rests in small groups. Nests in colonies on rocky islands throughout Mediterranean. Vocal at nest – loud cawing notes. Most depart in winter but may be seen offshore at any time.

YELKOUAN SHEARWATER *Puffinus yelkouan* 33cm

(Vulnerable) Elegant slim-winged shearwater, much smaller than Scopoli's, with strongly contrasting plumage. Upperparts dark brownish-black, underparts white, with dark wing edges and sometimes dusky sides to undertail. May show dusky half-stripe on base of underwing. Bill long, slim with hooked tip. Flight agile and dynamic, alternating long glides on stiff wings with rapid flapping, tilting to show dark upperside and white underside alternately. Also rests on sea surface. Nests in colonies in burrows, on islands throughout Mediterranean, coming ashore at night, when very vocal with loud, gargling or coughing calls. Ranges widely throughout the Mediterranean in winter, when may be seen offshore.

WHITE STORK *Ciconia ciconia* 104cm

Unmistakeable, robust large bird with long legs and neck, more stoutly built than herons or Spoonbill. Plumage white, with black flight feathers obvious both at rest and in flight. Legs and long heavy bill bright red (bill dark-tipped in juvenile), eye dark with narrow, short black eye-stripe. Flies with legs and neck outstretched. Quiet, but when reunited at nest pairs perform bill-clattering display. Forages on open ground, stalking prey on foot. Builds very large stick nest, often in towns or villages on prominent buildings; nests reused year on year, and small birds such as sparrows may nest within their structure. A localised summer visitor to Italy.

BITTERN *Botaurus stellaris* 75cm

A large, stocky and shy heron. Often looks squat with neck hunched. Plumage warm brown with darker streaks and spots. Long dark streaks on throat and breast provide camouflage when in characteristic head-raised posture in reedbed. Legs relatively short and thick, greenish, toes long. Eye pale with dark streak below, bill shortish, dull yellow. May be seen stalking along reedbed edges. Neck retracted in flight, broad brown wings giving owl-like impression, belied by projecting toes. Gives hoarse croak in flight, male's 'song' a hollow, breathy *boom*. Breeds in marshy wetlands with extensive reedbeds; winter wanderers may use smaller reedbeds. Localised resident.

▲ Adult male   ▲ Adult female

LITTLE BITTERN *Ixobrychus minutus* 35cm

Dainty heron (body size similar to Moorhen) with proportionally large head. Adult male light yellow-buff with black crown, back and flight feathers; contrasting pale wing-coverts forming large, prominent circular patch in flight. Female similar but drabber, less contrasting, and juvenile quite uniform streaky brown. Bill, legs and eye yellowish. Shy, keeps within cover and climbs among reeds and shrubs with great agility. Song a series of well-spaced low croaks; gives *kwek* call in flight. Builds nest from dead reeds, in thick cover and often above ground level. Prefers marshes with reedbeds, and wet sedgy meadows with scrub. A common but declining summer visitor.

33

NIGHT HERON *Nycticorax nycticorax* 62cm

Stocky smallish heron with thick neck and short body, shortish stout bill. Adult grey, paler below than above, with black back and crown, narrow white forehead stripe, and a few long pale plumes on back. Wings uniform grey in flight. Eye red, bill black, legs yellow (becoming pinker at start of breeding season). Juvenile very different – mid-grey-brown on upperside with heavy pale spotting, underside creamy with heavy buff streaks; eye, leg and bill dull. Has short croaking flight call. Most active at night; may forage in small groups. Found in wetlands, nesting colonially in trees or reedbeds. Fairly common summer visitor, scarce and localised in winter.

▽ Adult   ▽ Juvenile

▲ Adult breeding

▲ Juvenile

SQUACCO HERON *Ardeola ralloides* 45cm

A small, pale, thick-necked heron. In breeding plumage yellowish-buff with browner streaked head and back, long dark-edged head-plumes. Bill blue-grey with black tip, eye pale, legs pinkish. Reveals entirely white wings and tail in flight; could be mistaken for an egret if not seen clearly. In winter, browner, more heavily streaked, bare parts much duller; juvenile similar. Has harsh duck-like flight call. Usually forages alone at water's edge or on floating vegetation, waiting to strike at fish or amphibians. Nests in small colonies in bushes or trees, feeds at marshes, well-vegetated lakes, rivers and other wetlands. A somewhat localised summer visitor.

CATTLE EGRET *Bubulcus ibis* 48cm

A small, thickset egret with short bill and full-looking chin, giving distinctly different outline to Little Egret. Plumage all white, with adults developing bright yellowish patches on crown, breast and back in the breeding season. Bill yellow (pinkish when breeding), eye pale, legs pale yellow-grey. Juvenile has dark bill with yellowish base. Flight call a soft croak. Gregarious, very often seen in fields with cattle or horses, preying on insects attracted by the livestock's droppings or disturbed as they forage; also found in wet marshland. Nests colonially in trees. Patchily distributed but locally common breeding bird in Italy, wandering a little more widely in winter.

▼ Adult breeding

▼ Adult non-breeding

GREY HERON *Ardea cinerea* 90cm

Tall, slender heron. Plumage grey with whiter underside, black streaks on throat, white crown, broad black supercilium extending into fine elongated black plumes dangling beside the neck. Bill and legs yellowish (brighter when breeding), eye pale. Juvenile has solid dark grey crown and duller bill and legs. Flies with retracted neck, forming prominent bulge, broad-winged and ponderous in flight. Loud harsh croaking call. Hunts at water's edge, waiting for prey or slowly stalking, also in fields; takes very diverse prey. Nests in colonies in treetops, may also forage in loose groups in wetlands. Fairly shy. Resident in northern Italy and Sicily, wandering more widely in winter.

PURPLE HERON *Ardea purpurea* 80cm

Smaller, darker and slimmer than Grey Heron, with strikingly long, thin, snake-like neck and long slim bill. Adult dark blue-grey with reddish-brown tints to forewings, thighs, neck-sides and face. Front of neck and breast marked with heavy dark streaks. Bill, eyes and legs yellowish. In flight the retracted neck forms prominent, angular bulge, toes often spread. Flight call a dry, brief croak. Hunting behaviour similar to Grey Heron's, usually shyer and quicker to flush. Builds stick nest in tree or bush, forms colonies. Found in marshes, reedbeds and wet meadows with ditches. A summer visitor and widespread passage migrant.

GREAT EGRET *Ardea alba* 92cm

Very tall white heron, close to Grey Heron in size but much slimmer build with very long, slender neck – outline helps distinguish from occasional leucistic Grey Heron. In breeding plumage develops long, fringed white plumes or 'aigrettes' on back and on lower breast. Bill yellow (darker in breeding season, with bluish base), feet and legs blackish (developing red tint on upper tibia when breeding). In flight shows very prominent neck bulge, long legs and feet stretching well beyond tail. Rarely calls (except at breeding colonies). Visits marshy wetlands and reedbeds. Scarce and localised breeding bird, but increasing; widespread on migration and in winter.

LITTLE EGRET *Egretta garzetta* 60cm

Smallish, slender white heron with long, slim neck, but often rests in tightly hunched, 'neck-less' posture. In breeding plumage develops long fine head-plumes and 'aigrettes' on back and front of breast. Bill dark, with pinkish base when breeding. Legs black, but feet bright yellow (however, may look dark when bird is foraging in muddy substrate). Eye pale. Flight call a harsh squawk. Hunts in shallow water at lake shore, using curious 'leg-jiggling' action to disturb prey; also forages by ditches and in fields. Nests colonially in trees. Resident mainly in parts of northern Italy and Sicily, passage migrant or winter visitor elsewhere.

AFRICAN SACRED IBIS *Threskiornis aethiopicus* 68cm

A tall, sturdy ibis with long, strong, down-curved black bill and long black legs. Dirty white with black head, neck and rear. Shows black edge to wing in flight; flies with neck and legs outstretched. Juvenile like adult but dark parts paler sooty grey-black with white speckles. Forages on ground, in open country, and is often attracted to rubbish tips. Sometimes utter harsh croak in flight. Gregarious when feeding. Nests in colonies on ground with nests close together, guarded by all adults. Established in Europe from zoo escapees, has bred in north-west Italy since 1989; increasing and present throughout northern Italy.

EURASIAN SPOONBILL *Platalea leucorodia* 86cm

Graceful long-legged wading bird with unique long, broad, spoon-shaped bill. Adult white, with yellow tint on neck and long shaggy crest in breeding plumage. Legs black, bill blackish becoming yellowish towards tip, dark lores. Juvenile has pinkish bill, white lores giving more 'open' expression, greyish legs, and shows black tips to primaries in flight. Flies with neck and legs extended. Sleeps in more horizontal position than Great Egret. Feeds by wading (up to belly-deep) and swishing bill through water. Gregarious. Generally silent. Found on marshes, lagoons and other wetlands. Scarce breeding bird but widespread passage migrant in Italy.

GLOSSY IBIS   *Plegadis falcinellus*   60cm

Elegant, long-necked but somewhat short-legged dark ibis, its outline recalling oversized Curlew. Often looks plain black at any distance. Breeding adult shows reddish-violet gloss and white at bill base, winter-plumaged adult and juvenile duller, with faint greenish gloss and white-speckled head and neck. Long down-curved bill dull yellowish, legs dull greenish. Flies with neck and legs outstretched; short tail with well-projecting feet. Generally quiet, but sometimes gives soft rolling grunt *krrrru*. Forages in shallows or in grassland, hunting frogs and large insects. Gregarious when feeding, and nests colonially in trees and reedbeds. Localised summer visitor; more widespread in winter and on migration.

NORTHERN GANNET   *Morus bassanus*   93cm

▲ *Adult* ▼ *Juvenile*

A large seabird with long, narrow, pointed wings and tapered, cigar-shaped body with stout pointed bill and pointed tail. Adult white with solid black wingtips, yellow flush to head, bill and eyes grey-blue, feet black. Juvenile entirely dark brown with fine white speckles, gradually acquiring white plumage (first on body, then wings) over four years. Gives harsh grating calls at the nest, otherwise silent. Breeds in colonies on inaccessible clifftops and islands. Feeds on fish caught after spectacular vertical plunge-dive; will swim on surface. Seen quite commonly offshore year-round, and a few pairs breed in Liguria region.

SHAG *Phalacrocorax aristotelis* 72cm

A sleek, dark, primitive-looking seabird. Short legs, long neck and long pointed tail. Blackish with green gloss, and dark feather fringes on back give scaly appearance. Develops curling upright crest at start of breeding season. Eyes green, bill and legs dark, shows small but conspicuous patch of yellow skin around gape. Juvenile paler, duller, with whitish chin and belly. Slimmer than Cormorant with finer bill, steeper forehead. Gives low grunts at nest. Swims low in water, begins dive with high porpoise-like leap. On land stands upright, often holds wings spread. Found in sheltered bays and further offshore, particularly in the north, very uncommon inland. A rare breeder and winter visitor.

▲ *Juvenile*

CORMORANT *Phalacrocorax carbo* 84cm

Larger, more robust than Shag with thicker bill. Adult blackish with bluish gloss (brown on wings), and white chin (duller in winter). In breeding season shows white flank patch and variable fine white feathers (filoplumes) on head and neck. Juvenile dull grey with almost white underparts. Low profile when swimming; slight jump before diving. Gives low croaking calls around nest. Catches large fish, which it swallows at the surface. Rests on land with wings spread to dry. Colonial nester; hunts alone but often seen flying in small groups. May be found at fish-rich inland lakes as well as at sea. Localised breeding resident; much more widespread in winter.

▶ *From top: adult, immature, adult breeding*

STONE-CURLEW *Burhinus oedicnemus* 41cm

Distinctive large-headed, long-tailed wader of dry open countryside. Plumage light brown with heavy, coarse dark streaking, pale stripes above and below eye, pale dark-edged wing-band, white belly and pale underwings with dark edge. Juvenile less boldly marked. In flight shows black flight feathers with white patches. Bill short, dark with yellow base. Eyes golden, very large. Legs yellow. Call a Curlew-like *kur-leee*, song (given at night) extended series of wailing notes. Forages and nests on all kinds of open, sparsely vegetated ground, relying on camouflage to avoid detection. Mainly nocturnal. A fairly widespread but scarce summer visitor.

OYSTERCATCHER *Haematopus ostralegus* 42cm

(Near Threatened) Distinctive, conspicuous and noisy shorebird. Robust, stocky build. Black upperside, head and breast, white belly and undertail. Develops narrow white throat-collar in winter. In flight shows broad white wing-bar, tail base, rump and lower back. Bill long, straight and bright orange (with dusky tip in winter), stout legs pink, eye red. Juvenile patterned like adult but sooty-grey above, bare parts duller. Loud ringing, piping calls. Feeds on seashore and rocks, breaking or prising molluscs open with its strong bill. Mainly on rocky or sandy beaches but sometimes on lake or river shores inland. Scarce summer visitor in north-east Italy, passage migrant or winter visitor elsewhere.

AVOCET *Recurvirostra avosetta* 44cm

Unmistakeable, elegant wader with unique upswept bill. Plumage mainly white, with black crown and hind-neck, black wing-markings and primaries. Bill thin, black, with strong up-curve; legs long, greyish. Juvenile like adult but dark areas paler. Chick grey with short, straight bill. Call a series of loud, ringing notes. Feeds very actively, sweeping bill side to side; wades in deep water, sometimes swims and even up-ends. Sociable, feeds and flies in flocks, nests colonially on lagoon islands and shores, with entire colony rising to fiercely mob any intruder. Breeds sparsely in northern Italy, also Sardinia and Sicily. Widespread at coast and inland on passage and in winter.

BLACK-WINGED STILT *Himantopus himantopus* 35cm

Unmistakeable slim wader with long pointed wings and preposterously long, bright candy-pink legs. White head and body, black back and wings, variable black or grey markings on head and hind-neck (some pure white). Bill mid-length, straight, black, very fine. Eye large, dark red. Juvenile similar but dark parts brownish, scaly-looking; dusky wash on face and hind-neck. Loud grating flight call, given very persistently at breeding colonies when mobbing intruders. Wades in deep water, picking food from surface. Nests on lake islands or shores, mainly near coast; migrants visit coastal marshland and lagoons. Widespread summer visitor and passage migrant, rare and local in winter.

▼ *Adult*   ▼ *Juvenile*

▲ Adult winter   ▲ Juvenile

GREY PLOVER *Pluvialis squatarola* 27cm

Rounded and robust, may recall miniature juvenile gull. In full breeding plumage (rare in Italy) has black face, breast and belly, silver-spangled upperparts, white breast-sides and neck-sides. In winter uniform dull mottled grey; juvenile similar but more brown-toned. Bill black, short and quite stout; eye large and dark, legs dark grey. In flight shows white wing-bar, and solid black patch in 'armpit'. Call a plaintive three-note whistle, *peee-uu-ee*. A shorebird, uncommon inland. Runs and pauses while foraging. Not especially gregarious, though often seen in ones or twos alongside other shoreline waders. Passage migrant and winter visitor.

GOLDEN PLOVER *Pluvialis apricaria* 26cm

Smaller, slimmer than Grey Plover with finer bill. In breeding plumage patterned like Grey Plover but white on breast-sides extends to flanks, and upperside washed golden. In winter, uniform dull yellowish-grey with fine speckling. Legs, bill and eyes dark. In flight shows hint of narrow white wing-bar; unlike Grey Plover, 'armpit' area white. Flight call single, slightly downslurred whistle. Agile on the wing, flocks seeming to sparkle white as they turn together. Feeds on damp grassland, marshes, lake shores, often in large flocks, much less frequent on beaches than Grey Plover. Widespread passage migrant and winter visitor to Italy.

▲ Adult breeding   ▲ Adult

RINGED PLOVER   *Charadrius hiaticula*   18cm

A plump, rounded small plover with bold markings. Upperside light brown, underside white, with broad black breast-band; black eye-stripe and forehead-band, eye dark without obvious eye-ring. Bill orange with black tip, legs orange. Black markings become dark brown and bare parts duller in winter, duller still in juvenile plumage. Shows narrow white wing-bar in flight. Call an upslurred whistle: *tuu-ip*. Runs and pauses before picking at the ground for food. Mainly a shorebird, foraging on sandy and stony beaches; less common inland but will visit lake shores and riversides. Usually in small flocks. A winter visitor and passage migrant in Italy; widespread.

LITTLE RINGED PLOVER   *Charadrius dubius*   17cm

Smaller and slighter than Ringed Plover, with clearly longer legs and rear end. Similar in colour and pattern, but breast-band narrower, has white line between black forehead-band and brown crown. Bold yellow eye-ring noticeable even at a distance. Legs dull pink, bill dark and slim. No obvious wing-bar in flight. Call a short downslurred *peeoo*. Forages on shoreline; in breeding season very active and vocal, chasing off rivals and potential predators; runs to and fro with flank feathers puffed out. Nests on gravel shores of lakes and lake islands, riversides or other bare ground near water. A common and widespread summer visitor and passage migrant.

▼ Adult breeding   ▼ Adult

KENTISH PLOVER *Charadrius alexandrinus* 16cm

Smaller and more lightly marked than Little Ringed Plover, with shorter rear end and proportionately large head. Male brown above and white below with narrow black broken breast-band, thin black eye-stripe, white supercilium, rufous tint on rear crown. Shows broad white wing-bar and rump-sides in flight. Bill slender and dark, legs dark. Female, non-breeding and juveniles paler and duller. Call a soft rolling purred whistle or an upslurred *tew-it*. Behaviour like other ringed plovers; often confiding. Nests on muddy or gravelly bare ground near water and close to coast (including on beaches). Scarce and declining resident, also passage migrant.

LAPWING *Vanellus vanellus* 30cm

(Near Threatened) Distinctive, attractive largish plover. Mainly white below, black above with green and violet gloss. Face partly white. Long, fine black crest. Undertail orange. In flight shows white underside to inner wings, white at primary tips. Wings round-ended, broad at 'hand' giving very distinctive wing shape; agile in the air with acrobatic tumbling territorial display flight. Juvenile duller with shorter crest. Legs pinkish, bill slim and black. Call a high, excitable two-note *pee-iich*; song a series of similar notes interspersed with wheezing, grating sounds. Feeds on grassland and open muddy ground in large flocks. Common winter visitor and passage migrant, resident in north.

WHIMBREL *Numenius phaeopus* 41cm

Largish wader, but smaller than Curlew. Plumage brown with fine dark streaks, dark feather centres on back and wings giving mottled pattern. Dark eye-stripe, pale supercilium and dark crown give stripy-faced impression. Bill longish with sharp bend about a third in from bill tip. Bill and legs dull grey. In flight shows white wedge on rump, all-dark wings with blackish primaries. Fast rippling flight call of about seven notes, all on same pitch. Visits mainly muddy shores on coast and inland around lakes, singly or in small groups. Passage migrant, mainly in north, more often seen in spring than autumn.

CURLEW *Numenius arquata* 54cm

(Near Threatened) Large, robust wader. Larger, longer-legged and longer-billed than Whimbrel (though smallest juvenile male Curlew very close in size and bill length to Whimbrel). Streaked and mottled brown, without Whimbrel's bold face stripes; eye prominent in rather plain head. Bill more smoothly down-curved than Whimbrel's; can be very long, with pinkish base. Legs grey. White rump wedge in flight, brown dark-tipped wings; can recall a juvenile large gull. Call melodious upslurred *coor-leee*. Usually seen in small groups or alone, foraging at stately pace on muddy shore or in shallow water, both coastal and inland. Widespread passage migrant and winter visitor; extremely rare and localised breeder in north-west.

BAR-TAILED GODWIT *Limosa lapponica* 36cm

(Near Threatened) Large, quite long-legged wader, with long slightly up-curved bill. In breeding plumage deep brick-red on head and underparts, including entire belly, dark eye-stripe and crown, mottled dark grey-brown on upperparts; bill dark. In winter pale grey-brown with heavily patterned upperparts, bill has pink base. Juvenile similar but with buff flush to face/breast. Legs dark. Shows barred tail and white rump wedge in flight; no wing-bar; pattern recalls Curlew. Call a sharp *kwee kwee*. Feeds on muddy lake- and seashores and in shallows; will wade in deep water. Seen singly or in small groups, a passage migrant mainly in northern Italy; rare and local in winter.

BLACK-TAILED GODWIT *Limosa limosa* 39cm

(Near Threatened) Longer-legged and more elegant than Bar-tailed Godwit. In breeding plumage orange-red on head and underside to breast, belly white with black barring, darkish eye-stripe and crown, lightly mottled grey-brown on upperside; bill dark at tip, orange-pink at base. In winter pale uniform grey-brown, whiter below. Juvenile similar but with peachy face/breast. In flight strongly patterned with broad white wing-bar on mostly black wings, black tail and square white rump patch. Call an abrupt, shrill three-note whistle. Feeds actively in shallow and deep water, more frequent in freshwater habitats than Bar-tailed; often forms large flocks. Widespread passage migrant, scarce winter visitor and rare and localised breeder in north west.

TURNSTONE *Arenaria interpres* 22cm

Distinctive stout, smallish shorebird. Has white underside and in breeding plumage (rare in Italy) boldly marked black and bright chestnut upperparts, fading to dark mottled grey-brown in winter, with blackish breast-band. Legs short, orange. Bill short, wedge-shaped, dark. In flight shows complex pattern – dark with white tail-band, back, wing-bar and shoulder-braces. Flight call a rattling chuckle. Feeds on stony and rocky shorelines (mainly seashore; uncommon inland), methodically exploring strandline and rocks, turning over stones to find sandhoppers; also scavenges strandline corpses. Often in small flocks; can be very approachable. Passage migrant and winter visitor, mainly on northern coasts.

RUFF *Calidris pugnax* 24–30cm (male larger)

Large, long-legged sandpiper with relatively short bill and small head. Breeding male sports large head-ruff and ear-tufts, varying in colour from white through various shades of barred buff, brown and rufous to black. Non-breeding male and female rather plain grey-brown with scaly back pattern produced by pale feather fringes. Often white around bill base. In flight shows narrow white wing-bar and rump-sides. Legs yellowish or orange, bill dark with orange base. Juvenile has dark bill, duller legs, warm buff plumage tone. Rarely calls. Feeds on shores in marshland and on wet grassland, also shores of lagoons and lakes. Widespread, sometimes abundant, passage migrant; rare and localised winter visitor.

▲ Adult autumn   ▲ Juvenile

CURLEW SANDPIPER *Calidris ferruginea* 20cm

(Near Threatened) Smallish, elegant and long-legged sandpiper, looks more rangy than Dunlin. In breeding plumage dark brick-red below, mottled blackish and grey above. In winter light silver-grey with clean white belly, dark lores and white eye-stripe. Juvenile similar but more scaly grey-brown above, with white belly, peachy breast and face. Shows thin white wing-bar and square white rump patch in flight. Legs dark, bill dark and longish with slight downward curve. Call a brisk harsh trill. Feeds on shore and in shallows in lagoons and lakes and on marshland. A widespread passage migrant, most numerous in late summer and autumn.

TEMMINCK'S STINT *Calidris temminckii* 14cm

Very small, rather plain sandpiper with short legs, horizontal posture. Grey-brown above, whitish below, some dark feather centres in breeding plumage but plainer and paler greyish outside breeding season; recalls miniature Common Sandpiper. Juvenile browner but with very plain appearance; lacks rufous tones and white shoulder-stripes of Little Stint. Long rear end, shortish straight bill, yellow or pale yellow-grey legs. Narrow white wing-bar and broad white tail-sides show in flight. Gives loud trilling flight-call when flushed. Feeds rather slowly with creeping action; unobtrusive. Usually seen singly. Feeds alongside fresh water including very small pools. Passage migrant and winter visitor.

▼ Adult breeding   ▼ Adult non-breeding

▲ Juvenile   ▲ Adult winter

SANDERLING *Calidris alba* 19cm

A compact, fast-running small sandpiper with a short, straight bill, notable for lacking a hind toe. Breeding plumage rather variable, with rather plain brownish or russet head and breast, spangled silver and brown upperparts and a white belly. In winter becomes very pale silvery-grey on upperside. In flight shows blackish forewing and black-edged white wing-bar. Bill and legs black. Flight call a sharp fluting *plip*. Usually seen foraging in small flocks on sandy shores at the surf edge, dashing back and forth in time with the breaking waves and picking up miniscule prey items. Passage migrant and winter visitor.

DUNLIN *Calidris alpina* 19cm

A small sandpiper with short legs and a fairly long, slightly down-curved bill, though size and bill length quite variable. In breeding plumage has large black belly patch and rufous mottling on back; upperparts otherwise streaked and speckled grey-brown, flanks white. Bill and legs dark. In winter plumage paler, greyer, with white belly. Juvenile like winter but browner, with some dark speckles on belly. In flight shows narrow pale wing-bar. Flight call a harsh purring or buzzing note. Often forms very large flocks, which forage mostly on muddy seashores and coastal lagoons. Moves more slowly than Sanderling. Widespread passage migrant and locally very common winter visitor.

▶ From top: adult autumn, adult winter, juvenile

▲ Adult

▲ Juvenile

LITTLE STINT *Calidris minuta* 15cm

Very small, short-billed sandpiper. In breeding plumage pale grey-brown or rufous-tinted above, white below, becoming paler and greyer in winter. Juvenile plumage (most likely in Italy) boldly patterned with dark eye-stripe, pale supercilium and prominent white shoulder-stripes; breast and belly white. Bill and legs dark. In flight shows narrow white wing-bar, broad white tail-sides. Call a short, sharp single note. Has more upright stance and faster feeding actions than similar-sized Temminck's Stint. Feeds on muddy shores around coastal lagoons and inland lakes, also on seashore and sometimes at edges of very small pools. Often associates with Dunlin. Passage migrant and winter visitor.

WOODCOCK *Scolopax rusticola* 35cm

Stout, long-billed, short-legged, short-necked and broad-winged wader. Plumage barred and dappled in shades of rich brown and grey, giving superb camouflage. Distinctive head with eyes set very far back and high up, long sloped forehead and peaked crown with transverse black bars, dark lores and cheek-stripe. Shows reddish rump in flight. Quiet except for territorial male's 'roding' flight at dusk, when he gives sporadic squeaking and croaking calls. Breeds in damp woodland with dense understorey; on migration may visit other habitats and even turn up in towns. Mainly winter visitor or passage migrant in Italy; resident in far north.

COMMON SNIPE   *Gallinago gallinago*   25cm

A compact, plump wader with shortish legs and very long, straight bill. Plumage intricately patterned in shades of brown, grey and cream; prominent yellowish shoulder-stripes. Dark eye-stripe, pale supercilium, dark crown with pale central stripe. Shows white belly and edges to secondaries in flight. When flushed gives abrupt rasping *scaap*, either singly or a series. Displaying male in flight produces bleating sound ('drumming') as air rushes through fanned tail feathers. Found in marshy habitats (upland and lowland) where it probes soft ground with long bill; difficult to spot on the ground. Mainly a common passage migrant and winter visitor in Italy, breeding in far north.

COMMON SANDPIPER   *Actitis hypoleucos*   19cm

A small sandpiper with shortish legs, slender build, and long tail. Light sandy grey-brown upperparts and mostly white underparts that extend in spur or gap around bend of wing. Legs greenish, bill fairly short, straight, brownish. In flight shows obvious white wing-bar. Flight action distinctive with series of fast, shallow wingbeats interrupted by glides on down-bowed wings. Call a penetrating short whistled *tsweee*, repeated in breathless series in territorial flight low over water. Walks with horizontal posture, constantly bobbing its rear end. Nests alongside rivers and lakes with gravelly shores in uplands and lowlands, not usually coastal. Widespread but scarce summer visitor, common passage migrant and winter visitor.

GREEN SANDPIPER *Tringa ochropus* 22cm

Larger, taller and darker than Common Sandpiper, with shorter tail and more upright stance; darker and more crisply marked than Wood Sandpiper. Upperparts dusky grey-brown with fine white speckles, changing in crisp line on breast to white underparts, with no white spur at wing-bend. White eye-ring. Bill longish, dark, legs dull grey-green. In flight shows broad bars on tail and neat white rump patch, wings solid dark both above and below. Flight call a clear, whistled *tlueet-wit-wit*. Usually feeds alone, working its way steadily along shorelines of lakes and ponds. A widespread passage migrant and winter visitor, some birds staying on through summer.

SPOTTED REDSHANK *Tringa erythropus* 31cm

An elegant slim wader with long legs and long bill with slightly drooping tip. In breeding plumage is entirely sooty blackish with fine white speckles, but transitions to very light grey winter plumage, with white belly and dark lores, white supercilium. Bill dark with a little red at base, legs red. Juvenile like winter-plumaged adult but darker, legs more orange. In flight shows long white patch on back. Call a clear, sharp, two-note *che-wit*. Feeds energetically in water up to belly-deep, immersing head or catching flies on the surface; mainly found on wetlands close to the coast. A widespread passage migrant, less commonly lingering through winter.

◄ *From top: adult spring, adult breeding, adult winter*

GREENSHANK *Tringa nebularia* 32cm

Large, elegant pale wader with proportionately rather large head. Plumage grey on upperside (darkest on wings), breast streaked, belly white. Head pale with prominent dark eye, bill dark, long and quite stout with slight upturn, long legs greenish. In flight shows dark wings and long white wedge extending well up back; tail white with faint dark barring. Call a loud *pew*, usually given in series of three notes. Feeds at water's edge and will wade belly-deep, occasionally swimming. Energetic; will chase small fish in shallows. Visits freshwater and coastal wetlands; widespread passage migrant, less commonly lingering through winter.

▷ *From top: adult breeding, adult winter flight, adult winter*

COMMON REDSHANK *Tringa totanus* 26cm

The most widespread *Tringa* sandpiper. Dusky grey-brown on upperparts, fading to paler on belly, underside very spotty in breeding plumage but more uniform in winter. Medium-long slim bill, red with darker tip. Legs longish, bright red (orange in juvenile). In flight shows prominent and unique broad white trailing edge to wing, and white wedge on back/rump. Call a sharp, ringing, slightly melancholic *teu* or *teu-teu*. Feeds on shorelines of lakes and rivers, also muddy seashores, probing for food and also flycatching in shallows. Nests on wet grassland. Resident and local as breeder, mainly in north-east; widespread passage migrant and fairly common winter visitor.

▽ *Adult breeding*

▽ *Adult winter*

WOOD SANDPIPER *Tringa glareola* 20cm

A slim, smallish and very dainty *Tringa* sandpiper, recalling slimmer, paler, more diffusely marked version of Green Sandpiper. Brownish on upperparts with pale spangling, this being especially pronounced in juveniles. Breast streaked brown, shading gradually into white belly. Head well-marked with dark eye-stripe and pale supercilium. Legs yellowish, slim straight bill grey, darker at tip. In flight shows all-dark wings and square white rump patch; tail has narrow dark barring. Call a high three-note whistle, *chiff-if-if*. Visits freshwater and saline marshland with pools, foraging at water's edge or wading. A very common and widespread passage migrant but unlikely to remain in winter.

COLLARED PRATINCOLE *Glareola pratincola* 26cm

Pratincoles are unusual waders, with plover-like plumage and tern-like body proportions – long wings and long forked tail. Collared Pratincole has grey-brown upperparts and breast, yellow lower breast shading to white belly, and yellow throat patch outlined in black. Juvenile has dark scaling on upperparts. Bill is short, stout and slightly down-curved, black at tip, red at base. Eye large, dark. Has graceful, agile flight, showing white rump, narrow white trailing edge to wing, and reddish-brown underwings. Call sharp, tern-like. Breeds colonially on flat open ground near water; hunts insect prey in air. A localised summer visitor and widespread passage migrant.

SLENDER-BILLED GULL   *Chroicocephalus genei*   40cm

A slim, pale, medium-sized gull with distinctive tapering head shape and long bill. Back and wings light grey, head and underparts white with pink tint in breeding season. Eye pale, legs red, bill dark red. Juvenile and subadult have paler bare parts, dark tail-tip and broad light brown wing-bar; never as boldly marked as same-aged Black-headed Gull. In flight wings show broad white leading edge and thin black trailing edge. Call harsh, low *kreeer*. Breeds in colonies on marshland and islands on coastal lagoons; usually scarcer than Black-headed Gull. Localised breeding bird in north-east, Apulia and Sardinia; more widespread on migration and in winter.

BLACK-HEADED GULL   *Chroicocephalus ridibundus*   37cm

The smallest gull breeding in the region. In summer has chocolate-brown hood not reaching nape, dark red bill, partial white eye-ring, dark eyes. Otherwise white with grey back and wings, dark wingtips. In winter bill red with black tip, head white with dark spot behind eye, faint dark bar above eye. Legs red (orange in subadults). Juvenile strongly chequered with warm ginger-brown upperparts. First-winter shows dark wing-bar and tail-tip. In flight (all ages) wing shows broad white leading edge and thin black trailing edge. Call loud, harsh downslurred screech. Nests in colonies on marshland and around lake shores and islands. Localised breeder, abundant and widespread passage migrant and winter visitor.

▼ *Adult summer*

▼ *Adult winter*

▲ Adult breeding ▲ Adult winter

MEDITERRANEAN GULL *Ichthyaetus melanocephalus* 39cm

Larger, more robust and stronger-billed than Black-headed. Breeding adult white with pale grey back and wings, white primaries, jet-black hood reaching nape, prominent white eye-ring. Bill red with black ring, legs red, eyes dark. In winter head white with dusky wash around eye. Looks very white in flight. Juvenile has black legs and bill, scaly grey-brown upperparts. First-winter has dark tail-tip and wing-bar, second-winter like adult but with trace of black in primaries. Call an interrogative rising-and-falling *kee-yow*. Breeds in colonies in similar habitats to Black-headed, often alongside it. Summer visitor in northeast; found around all coasts in winter.

56

AUDOUIN'S GULL *Ichthyaetus audouinii* 48cm

Rather dusky-looking medium-sized gull. Adult has white head and underside with pale grey wash, darker grey upperparts, black wingtips with white primary spots. Bill dark red, legs greenish-grey, eyes dark. Juvenile dark, scaly, sooty-grey all over, bill and legs greyish; develops whiter head and some paler grey on back by first-winter. In flight wings show only a very narrow white trailing edge. Gives various harsh, low-pitched nasal calls. Nests in colonies on rocky islands. Mainly hunts fish in shallows rather than scavenging. Uncommon resident on suitable islands around Italian coast, more widespread (especially in south) outside breeding season.

▲ Immature   ▲ Adult winter

LESSER BLACK-BACKED GULL *Larus fuscus* 52cm

Darker than Yellow-legged Gull in all plumages, a little smaller and distinctly slighter with longer wings. Adult has white head (streaked grey in winter) and underside, dark slate-grey back and wings, black wingtips with white spots. Bill yellow with red spot, legs yellow (duller in winter). Juvenile dark, rather uniform sooty-grey, black bill, dull pink legs, shows whitish rump in flight. Subadult gradually develops adult-type plumage over four years. Calls varied yelping, cackling and growling notes, very like those of Yellow-legged Gull. Forages on shorelines and will visit fields, rubbish dumps. Fairly uncommon passage migrant and winter visitor.

YELLOW-LEGGED GULL *Larus michahellis* 55cm

The most common large gull. Stout and robust with strong bill, rather short wings. Adult has white head (lightly streaked grey in winter) and underparts, mid-grey back and wings, black wingtips with white spots. Bill yellow with red spot, legs yellow. Juvenile streaked and mottled grey-brown with pale head, dark bill, pink legs. First-winter similar but paler, second-winter has plain grey back and whiter underside, third-winter like adult but with some brown remaining in wings and tail-tip. Calls include various low-pitched mews, cackles and grunts. Common coastal breeding bird, preferring rocky shores. Widespread in winter, including around towns.

▼ Adult   ▼ Immature

LITTLE TERN   *Sternula albifrons*   23cm

Very small, short-tailed, long-billed tern. Adult mid-grey above, white below, crown black with white forehead patch (larger in winter). Bill yellow with black tip (completely black in winter), legs reddish. In flight shows broad dark leading edge to long, narrow wings. Juvenile has dark bill, dull legs, dark barring on back and wings. Call very sharp, grating *krrreet*, extended into chattering series in alarm. Has erratic, jerky flight, mainly picks food from surface rather than plunge-diving. Nests colonially on sandy or gravelly seashores, or coastal rivers and lakes. Localised summer visitor, mainly in north-east and far south, may be seen offshore of all coasts on migration.

GULL-BILLED TERN   *Gelochelidon nilotica*   39cm

Robust, short-tailed, large tern, similar to rarer Sandwich Tern but darker with shorter and much stouter bill, and lacks crest. Adult white on underparts, mid-grey upperparts with darker wingtips, black crown extending down to hind-neck, bill and legs black. In winter head white with restricted dark mask around eye. Juvenile pale with no black cap but sandy tints on wings, neck and crown. Call disyllabic, low-pitched *gur-wick*. Graceful and relaxed flight, hawks insects and picks prey from water's surface but rarely plunge-dives. Nests in colonies on open flat ground near water, at coasts and inland. Very localised summer visitor and quite widespread passage migrant.

▼ *Adult breeding in flight*   ▼ *Adult breeding*

WHISKERED TERN *Chlidonias hybrida* 26cm

Largest and stoutest-billed of the three *Chlidonias* 'marsh' terns.
Breeding adult uniform dark grey with black crown and white face. Bill
and legs dark red. Winter adult much paler with whitish underparts
and white forehead patch. In flight shows shiny silver cast to
upperside of flight feathers. Underparts of body darker than uniform
light grey underwings. Tail short with shallow fork. Juvenile has white
underparts, coarse brownish scaling on back. Hawks and dips to water
for prey. Call a shrill single rasping note. Nests colonially on marshland
and shores of lakes and rivers. Rare, localised summer visitor to north-
east Italy; may be seen anywhere with suitable habitat on migration.

WHITE-WINGED BLACK TERN *Chlidonias leucopterus* 22cm

The smallest marsh tern. Dainty and small-billed. Adult black shading
to paler grey on back, strongly contrasting white forewings. In flight
shows white rump, black underwing. Bill black, legs dark red. In winter
white on head and underparts, light grey on upperparts, dark spot
behind eye and fine grey streaks on crown. Juvenile has dark back,
cheeks and hind-crown, white underparts, grey wings, more crisply
patterned than juvenile Black Tern. Call a soft low *kek* or harsher *chree*.
Agile and aerial, hawks and dips over water. Breeds irregularly in far
north-west of Italy but occurs as regular passage migrant.

BLACK TERN *Chlidonias niger* 24cm

Graceful, dark and long-billed marsh tern. Breeding adult black with grey back and wings. Bill black, legs blackish-red. In flight looks much plainer than White-winged Black Tern, with almost uniform grey upperside. Underwing grey, contrasting with black belly. In winter has white underparts and mostly white head with dark hind-crown and cheek, legs redder. Juvenile similar but with brownish pale-edged scaling on back, pinkish legs. Chattering flight call recalls Little Tern. Breeds on marshland, and on migration visits all kinds of open fresh water with plenty of insects; also sea coasts. Scarce, localised and declining breeder in north-west but common and widespread passage migrant.

COMMON TERN *Sterna hirundo* 35cm

Medium-sized, very long-tailed tern. Adult has light grey upperparts with darker wingtips, white head with neat black cap extending to nape, whitish-grey breast and belly. Bill red with black tip, legs short, red. In winter bill becomes darker, forehead white. Juvenile has heavy ginger-brown scaling on back and wings, orange-pink legs and bill-base. Call a short, sharp kik; also series of calls *kirri-kirri-kirri*. Very graceful on the wing, dips and plunge-dives for food. Nests in colonies on gravelly shores or islands, coastal and inland. Summer visitor in north and Sardinia, elsewhere a passage migrant, particularly on east coast.

SANDWICH TERN *Sterna sandvicensis* 40cm

Large tern with very long wings and shortish tail. Adult pearly grey on upperwings, with white head, breast and belly. Cap black, extended at back of crown into a short, shaggy crest. Bill long, black with yellow tip. Legs black. In winter has white forehead. Juvenile has dark barring on upperside, shorter bill and duskier crown than adult. First-winter retains a little dark barring and diffuse pale forehead patch. Call sharp upslurred *kerrr-ick*. Strong flier, performs spectacular plunge-dives from some height. Nests in colonies on sandy beaches or islands, usually coastal. Summer visitor in north-east, otherwise widespread passage migrant and winter visitor.

OSPREY *Pandion haliaetus* 56cm

Distinctive large, long-winged raptor. Dark brown upperparts, white below with variable brownish breast-band (heavier in females). Head white with broad dark eye-stripe, shaggy crest at rear of crown. Bill and legs grey, eyes yellow. Juvenile has pale feather fringes on upperparts, giving scaly look; dull orange eyes. In flight underwing shows barred flight feathers, dark wrist patch. Has relaxed powerful flapping flight, recalling large gull. Gives yelping calls around nest, otherwise quiet. Hovers and dives to catch fish, sometimes fully submerging before surfacing with prey in talons. Hunts at lakes and sea coasts. Rare summer visitor, mainly north-west, and widespread passage migrant.

▲ *Adult in flight* ▼ *Adult*

EUROPEAN HONEY-BUZZARD *Pernis apivorus* 55cm

Large raptor, superficially similar to Common Buzzard, with longer and narrower wings and tail, longer neck and more projecting head. Very variable. Adult typically light brown shading to grey on head, underparts mottled. Feet and eyes yellow, bill relatively small and long. Tail has broad bars at base and tip with wide gap between. Juvenile very like Common Buzzard; dark-eyed, plumage varies from pale through rufous and grey-brown to very dark. Gives whistling calls near nest. Breeds in woodland with open countryside nearby. Feeds mainly on wasp larvae, and not able to take large prey. A very widespread though shy summer visitor and passage migrant.

SHORT-TOED EAGLE *Circaetus gallicus* 65cm

▲ Adult ▼ Juvenile

A large, stocky, big-headed raptor, long-winged and short-tailed. Fairly uniform brown above and pale with variable barring below; pale and darker forms exist. In flight often looks very pale from below, with clear-cut darker breast and head. Underwing shows evenly spaced barring with no obvious dark patch at wrist; tail has three or four well-spaced bars. Bill and feet grey, eye yellowish-orange. Has fluting call when breeding. Searches in soaring flight for prey, mainly snakes and lizards. Often hovers before pounce. Breeds in open, often rugged countryside with some trees. A fairly widespread summer visitor and passage migrant.

GRIFFON VULTURE *Gyps fulvus* 100cm

A huge bird of prey with dull sandy-brown plumage, head and long neck downy white, whitish neck-ruff. Eyes dark, bill yellow. Juvenile has grey bill and brownish ruff. In flight shows very long, broad wings with outer primaries separated as long 'fingers'; flight feathers and tail dark brown. Makes hisses and grunting sounds at nest and gathered at carcass. Prefers rugged countryside with mountainsides to generate thermals; feeds on carrion. Breeds in Sardinia but increasingly seen throughout Italy because of reintroduction projects, with new breeding colonies established from the Alps south to central and south Italy and Sicily.

GOLDEN EAGLE *Aquila chrysaetos* 86cm

Very large, imposing and majestic raptor, well-proportioned with long wings and relatively long tail, orange eyes. Adult (5+ years old) dark grey-brown with bright reddish-orange streaks on head and neck, some paler yellowish feathers on forewing, forming vague bar in flight. Juvenile more uniform warm dark brown; in flight shows large white wing patch at primary bases; white areas gradually shrink with successive moults. Generally quiet, but may give soft whistling call. Soars easily on thermals and skims along crag edges, searching for prey or carrion. Adult pairs hold large territory over many years; subadults wander. Prefers remote mountainous areas with some forest. Widespread resident in uplands.

 ▲ Adult dark morph ▲ Adult light morph

BOOTED EAGLE *Aquila pennata* 46cm

A small, buzzard-sized eagle with long wings and longish, square-cut tail. Adult occurs in dark, pale and intermediate morphs. All forms rather uniform brown (sandy, reddish or dark) with slight darker streaking on upperparts and underparts. Eyes pale, legs feathered, feet yellow. In flight from below, pale morph shows strong contrast between pale body and forewing and dark flight feathers; darker forms show black bar on mid-wing. Upperwing shows pale mid-wing patch. Noisy when breeding, shrill *klee klee* calls and buzzard-like mews. Soars to search for prey, stoops sharply to catch it on ground. Found in open country and lightly wooded areas; uncommon passage migrant and winter visitor. A few birds oversummer in south.

MARSH HARRIER *Circus aeruginosus* 49cm

The largest and stockiest harrier. Long-winged and long-tailed. Male tricoloured, with light grey head, body, tail and outer parts of wings, red-brown back, belly and inner wings, large black primary patch, eye pale. Female and juvenile very dark brown with variable creamy crown, chin and shoulders, tail a shade paler, eyes dark. Generally silent, but may produce quiet whistles or chattering near nest. Hunts in low, steady patrolling flight over vegetation, listening and watching for prey moving on ground. Mainly found in marshland, reedbeds, wet pasture, but also sometimes farmland. Resident in north, passage migrant and winter visitor further south.

◄ From top: adult male, adult female, immature female

▲ *Adult male*   ▲ *Adult female*

HEN HARRIER   *Circus cyaneus*   **50cm**

More lightly built than Marsh Harrier, with longer wings and tail. Male light grey, paler below, with large black wingtips and white rump, eyes yellow. Juvenile and adult female streaky grey-brown, brighter and warmer-toned in juvenile, with white rump, bold dark bars on tail, pale outline to facial disc; eyes dark in juvenile, paler in adult female. Quiet away from breeding grounds. Very light, buoyant low flight, locating prey on ground mainly by sound. Hunts over well-vegetated open countryside, farmland, meadows, heathland, marshes. Forms communal roosts in winter and on migration. A widespread passage migrant and winter visitor.

MONTAGU'S HARRIER   *Circus pygargus*   **45cm**

The smallest harrier. Very long-winged and elegant; shows four 'fingers' on wingtips in flight (five in Hen Harrier). Male grey with very large area of black on wingtips, narrow white rump patch, faint reddish streaks on lower belly. In flight shows conspicuous single black wing-bar on both upperparts and underparts, with adjacent reddish barring on underwing. Female like female Hen Harrier, but juvenile much more rufous and uniform on underparts than juvenile Hen Harrier. Gives whistling and chattering calls near nest. Found in open countryside, arable farmland, meadows, marshland. A summer visitor, more common in north, and passage migrant throughout Italy.

▽ *Adult female*   ▽ *Adult male*

▲ Adult female in flight   ▲ Adult female

SPARROWHAWK *Accipiter nisus* 32–38cm

A small raptor (but female much larger and heavier than male), long-tailed and broad-winged. Adult male blue-grey above, brick-red on cheeks and breast, becoming barred red on whitish belly. Adult female grey-brown above; underside pale, heavily barred darker, may have hint of red on cheeks and flanks. Juvenile brown with pale fringes on upperparts, very coarse brown barring on underparts. Eye yellow (becoming redder in older males). Gives chattering calls near nest. Hunting flight alternates fast flaps and short glides; also soars, especially early in breeding season. Hunts birds, making surprise attack after low approach flight behind cover. Found in woodland, parks, gardens. A widespread resident.

GOSHAWK *Accipiter gentilis* 52–61cm

A large, very powerful raptor. Female much larger than male. Adult dark grey-blue above, whitish below with fine darker barring, white supercilium and undertail. Eye orange. Juvenile brown, pale yellowish below with heavy dark vertical streaks; eye yellow. In flight markedly stockier than Sparrowhawk with large pro-truding head, round-ended rather than square-cut tail, distinct 'bulge' to trailing edge of secondaries. Quiet but may give cackling call near nest. Has fast low hunting flight; in courtship soars with white undertail puffed out. Hunts birds and mammals. Prefers undisturbed woodland with areas of open countryside nearby. A fairly widespread (but shy) resident, wandering more widely in winter.

RED KITE *Milvus milvus* 66cm

(Near Threatened) Large but relatively lightweight raptor with long wings, unique long, deeply forked tail. Plumage warm rufous-brown with dark feather centres on upperparts, creating mottled appearance; dark streaks on underparts. Head greyish with darker streaks. Eyes pale. Underwing dark with black wingtip and pale 'window' at primary bases. From above tail looks very red, almost unmarked. Call a buzzard-like but weak mewing. Agile in flight, soars and glides, twisting tail to steer. Feeds mainly on carrion and invertebrates; may gather in large numbers at suitable foraging grounds. Open countryside with areas of woodland. A widespread resident in south, passage migrant and winter visitor further north.

BLACK KITE *Milvus migrans* 53cm

Like Red Kite but smaller, with shorter tail and duller, less contrasting plumage. Adult almost uniform grey-brown, eye pale. Juvenile has dark eye, mottled upperparts, suggestion of dark eye-mask. In flight, underwing shows vague paler window at primary bases. Tail only slightly forked; looks square-ended when fanned out. Gives mewing and whistling calls. Graceful on the wing though a little more laboured than Red Kite. Often seen in large gatherings; visits ploughed fields to take worms, and joins crows and gulls at rubbish dumps; also scavenges around fisheries. Found in town and countryside, nests in woodland. A common, widespread summer visitor and passage migrant.

COMMON BUZZARD *Buteo buteo* 52cm

Large, familiar raptor, compact with broad wings and short tail. Plumage basically mottled dull brown but highly variable, from almost white to extremely dark. Most individuals dark brown with a more or less prominent paler breast-band. Tail evenly barred, underwing shows dark feather tips and dark patch at wrist-bend (prominent in pale birds). Eye dark (paler in juvenile). Gives mournful, far-carrying mewing call. Soars easily on thermals, often in groups; also often seen resting on low posts. Very diverse diet, including carrion and live prey (vertebrates and invertebrates). Found in open, mainly lowland countryside with some trees. Common and widespread resident.

BARN OWL *Tyto alba* 36cm

A slim, pale owl with long wings and legs. Upperparts mottled golden and grey, underparts white or with buff wash (female typically darker). Long oval or heart-shaped facial disc white, with thin dark border. Eyes black, relatively small. In flight can look ghostly; underwing pale and almost unmarked. Call a harsh, hoarse scream. Has buoyant, slow hunting flight, turning and hovering often before dropping down with legs outstretched. Active mainly at night but sometimes in daylight. Hunts small mammals, which it locates by sound. Prefers open country with some derelict buildings or old trees with holes for nesting. Common resident.

LITTLE OWL *Athene noctua* 25cm

Small stocky owl with short wings and tail, and broad, flat-topped head. Upperside grey-brown with white spots (small on crown, large on back and wings). Underparts pale with darker streaking. Has large yellow eyes under frowning white supercilia. Facial disc not well-defined. Juvenile more uniform in plumage tones, with unspotted crown. Has bounding flight pattern. Call a high-pitched two-note *kyew*. Hunts all kinds of small prey, pouncing from a perch or chasing on the ground. Most active in early evening but often seen resting in daylight on prominent perch. Found in open countryside; farmland, scrub, gardens and similar; often nests in old buildings. Common resident.

SCOPS OWL *Otus scops* 20cm

Very small, slender owl with ear-tufts. Plumage tone varies from rufous-brown to greyer, but always finely and intricately patterned; superbly camouflaged against tree bark. Eyes yellow. Face and body shape and prominence of ear-tufts changes drastically with bird's state of alertness – at rest becomes tall and slim with tufts fully raised. Male's song a soft, tuneful purring note, repeated constantly. Strictly nocturnal, resting in cover by day. Feeds mainly on insects, hunts by pouncing from a perch. Found in all kinds of wooded areas including town parks and gardens, often nests in old woodpecker holes. A widespread, common summer visitor, resident in far south.

LONG-EARED OWL *Asio otus* 34cm

Largish, slim owl with long wings and prominent ear-tufts. Upperparts grey-brown, mottled and speckled darker, with line of white spots on shoulder. Underparts buff with heavy dark streaks. Facial disc well-defined, rufous with whitish brows and bill base, eyes orange. Fledglings leave nest early; downy grey with black face. In flight ear-tufts held flat. Orange patch at primary bases on upperwing; underwing paler with black mark at bend. Territorial song is repeated short, deep hoots; begging chicks make 'squeaky-gate' noises. Hunts small vertebrate prey in flight at night. Usually nests in old birds' nests. Prefers forest edges, plantations, and other habitats combining trees and open ground. Widespread resident.

TAWNY OWL *Strix aluco* 40cm

Fairly large, big-headed owl. Plumage cryptically patterned with mottling and streaks, base colour greyish, brown or rufous. Facial disc rather plain, black eyes prominent. Young leave nest early, still flightless; rather plain grey and very fluffy. Very round-winged in flight, shows evenly barred flight feathers and no obvious dark marking at wing-bend. Song a long, fluting, quavering hoot, call a sharp *ke-vick*. Hunts mainly from perch, takes great variety of prey. Sedentary and territorial. Found in woodland, uses large tree hole for nesting. A common resident, but absent from far south-east and Sardinia.

HOOPOE *Upupa epops* 27cm

Unmistakeable, medium-sized bird with long crest and long, slender down-curved bill. Head and body plumage soft pinkish-buff, wings and tail boldly patterned in black and white. Crest usually held swept back to form point, but can be raised and spread; each feather tipped black. In flight looks very broad-winged, giving butterfly-like impression. Song a three-note hoot, also various harsh rolling calls. Catches insect prey on ground. Surprisingly inconspicuous when moving slowly in dappled shadow. Prefers short grassland for foraging but needs tree hole or crevice in building for its nest. A common and widespread summer visitor.

WRYNECK *Jynx torquilla* 17cm

A small, rather peculiar woodpecker. Plumage beautifully patterned, with grey head, back and tail, brown wings, all with darker stripes and bars. Throat buff, fading to whitish on belly, finely barred. Bill small, tail long with widely spaced dark bars. Song a series of well-spaced single loud *kee* whistles; also gives sharp *tec* call. Does not climb tree trunks using tail as prop, but tends to forage on ground, searching for ants, hopping in thrush-like manner. Uses existing tree holes for nest, rather than making its own. Found in all kinds of countryside with some trees and some grassland. Widespread summer visitor.

GREEN WOODPECKER *Picus viridis* 33cm

A large, rangy-looking woodpecker. Body plumage dull olive-green, paler grey-green on underparts. Crown and hind-neck bright red. Black patch around eye and broad black stripe reaching back from bill base; red-centred in male, solid black in female. Eye pale. Juvenile very spotty, lacks black on face. Bill large, strong, dull horn-grey. In flight shows vivid yellow-gold rump, and barred flight and tail feathers. Call a loud series of yelping, laughing notes. Seldom drums – drumming roll quiet, lasts 1.5 seconds. Feeds mainly on ants, hops on the ground. Lives in open countryside with some mature trees for nesting. A common, widespread resident, but absent from Sicily and Sardinia.

BLACK WOODPECKER *Dryocopus martius* 43cm

Very large woodpecker; crow-sized but different shape with long slim neck, slight shaggy crest at rear of crown giving angular head-shape, pointed tail. Plumage black except for red crown in male, red hind-crown patch in female. Eye and bill pale. Looks elongated in flight, and flies directly rather than bounding like smaller woodpeckers. Various loud ringing calls, and very loud far-carrying drumming in 2–3-second bursts. Forages mainly on tree branches and trunks, excavating grubs from rotting wood. Nest-hole oval, 12cm across at widest point. Found in mature forest. Common in Alps, scarce in Apennines and far south, absent from Sicily and Sardinia.

LESSER SPOTTED WOODPECKER *Dendrocopos minor* 15cm

Very small, short-billed and compact black-and-white woodpecker. Black upperparts with broad white bars across back and wings. Underparts whitish with fine dark streaks; no red undertail. Head white with black stripe from bill base curving around cheek; crown red with black border in male, solid black in female. Call is weaker version of Great Spotted's, also a series of ringing notes, recalling Wryneck. Drumming soft, slower than Great Spotted's, in 1.2–1.8-second bursts. Not especially shy, but discreet. Climbs and forages along thin high twigs as well as broader boughs, and may join foraging flocks of tits. Fairly common widespread woodland resident, but not on Sicily or Sardinia.

GREAT SPOTTED WOODPECKER *Dendrocopos major* 24cm

Starling-sized black-and-white woodpecker with strong bill. Black upperparts with white bars on wings and long oval patch on shoulders. Undertail red. Head white with black crown and stripes on lower face, enclosing white cheek. Male has red patch at hind-crown. Juvenile has red crown (more extensive in male juveniles) and pink undertail. Call a sharp *kik*, series of longer grating notes in territorial dispute. Drumming lasts less than 1 second, beats very fast, blending into single 'creaking' sound. Feeds in trees, breaking into decaying wood to access grubs. Woodland, particularly mixed with some spruce and pine. Common, widespread resident including Sicily and Sardinia.

EUROPEAN BEE-EATER *Merops apiaster* 27cm

Spectacular, unmistakeable multicoloured bird, slim and elongated with large head. Blue underparts and flight feathers, orange-brown upperparts with yellow shoulders, yellow throat outlined in black. Bill long, down-curved, eye red. Central tail feathers protrude as long spike. Juvenile a little paler and drabber, green tinted on upperparts. Very graceful in flight, pointed wings are pale underneath with black trailing edge. Call a pleasant rolling *prrrt*. Catches insect prey on the wing. Gregarious, nests in colonies in burrows dug into sand-banks or riversides. Open scrubby countryside in warm lowlands with plenty of insect life. A widespread summer visitor.

ROLLER *Coracias garrulus* 31cm

Robust bird with large head, strong bill. Somewhat crow-like in shape, but dazzlingly colourful. Body and most of wings bright iridescent turquoise-blue. Back and inner parts of wing bright chestnut. In flight looks Jackdaw-shaped, flight feathers blackish above, dark blue below. Tail has dark base and black corners. Eye and bill black. Juvenile is duller, paler version of adult. Call and alarm are harsh crow-like notes. Hunts insects and small vertebrates, often watching for prey from perch on overhead wire. Habitat open countryside with some trees; usually nests in tree-hole. Patchily distributed summer visitor, more widespread on migration.

KINGFISHER *Alcedo atthis* 18cm

Compact, very colourful bird. Short-tailed, long-billed and very short-legged. Upperparts blue-green with fine paler spots; rump and back dazzling iridescent light sky-blue. Underparts orange. White stripe on neck-side and white chin, orange patch behind eye, head otherwise blue-green. Bill dark, with red on lower mandible in female. Eyes dark, feet red. Juvenile slightly duller with dark feet, patchy brownish breast-band. Call a high, piercing single whistle. Preys on fish and other aquatic animals which it catches with plunge-dive from perch or from hovering. Nests in bankside tunnel. Found around rivers and lakes, sometimes sheltered sea coasts. Common, widespread resident.

LESSER KESTREL *Falco naumanni* 30cm

Small, elegant, long-tailed falcon. Adult male has solid blue-grey head, wing panel and tail, unmarked chestnut back and forewing, black tail-band and primaries. Chin white, underparts light buff with fine dark spots. Female chestnut above with black spotting, paler below with dark streaks, tail banded. Eyes dark, feet yellow, claws white (black in Kestrel). In flight shows long pointed wings, central tail feathers slightly longer. Has distinctive rasping three-note call. Hunts insects and small vertebrates, hovering before dropping down. Gregarious, nests in loose colonies, mainly in old buildings (including in towns), hunting in nearby open countryside. Uncommon but increasing summer visitor, mainly in south.

▶ *From top: adult male, adult male perched, adult female*

▲ *Adult female*
▶ *Adult male*

COMMON KESTREL *Falco tinnunculus* 34cm

A little larger and stouter than Lesser Kestrel. Long-tailed and somewhat broad-winged. Male has grey tail with black terminal band, and grey head with dark, narrow moustachial stripe. Upperside chestnut with black spotting, underside light buff with dark spots. Female chestnut on upperparts with strong black barring, underparts pale, streaked darker. Tail banded. Call a series of short, sharp *kee* notes. Has fast flapping flight but also soars; hovers when hunting, preys mainly on small vertebrates, some large insects. Less gregarious than Lesser Kestrel. Hunts over grassland, farmland, road verges. Nests in tree hollow or crevice in building. Common, widespread resident.

RED-FOOTED FALCON *Falco vespertinus* 31cm

(Near Threatened) A small falcon with distinctive and unique plumage. Male is uniform dark slaty grey except for thighs and undertail, which are dark reddish. Female has dark grey back and wings, with black chequering, a white face with dark eye-mask and moustachial stripe, and rich orange-buff crown and underparts. Legs and eye-ring red. Juvenile like paler, browner version of juvenile Hobby. Call, given around nest, is a fast chatter: *kekekeke*. Hawks insects in flight, Hobby-like, but also hovers and catches prey on ground in manner of a kestrel. A summer visitor to Po Valley; also fairly common and widespread passage migrant.

▼ *Adult male*   ▼ *Adult female*

▲ *Adult dark morph*
◀ *Adult light morph*

ELEONORA'S FALCON *Falco eleonorae* 39cm

Fairly large, long-tailed and very long-winged falcon. Adult has two colour morphs – dark (uniform brownish-black) and pale (dark upperparts, white cheeks, red-brown underparts with dark streaks). Juvenile is greyer, scalier version of pale adult. Call repeated sharp, grating *keh* calls. Fast flickering flight, very agile, catches small birds on wing over open sea. Nests in colonies on rocky islets and sea cliffs. Begins breeding cycle very late in summer, so chick-rearing coincides with peak passerine migration through region. A summer visitor, present well into autumn, most numerous around Sicily and Sardinia.

HOBBY *Falco subbuteo* 32cm

Close to Kestrel in size but with much longer, narrower wings. Adult dark slate-grey above with white chin and cheeks, narrow black moustachial stripe and shorter black 'spur' behind, creating distinctive face pattern. Underparts pale with heavy, neat black streaks; underwing heavily chequered. Undertail and thighs rufous-red. Juvenile similar but browner, upperparts scaly, face more dusky, buff rather than red undertail and thighs. Call comprises ringing *kew kew* notes. Agile, tireless wheeling flight, recalling a swift; catches and eats large insects on the wing. Hunts over open ground, marshes, heaths. Nests in old birds' nest in tree. A fairly widespread summer visitor and passage migrant.

▶ *From top: adult, adult perched, juvenile*

LANNER FALCON
Falco biarmicus 47cm

A rather dark falcon, a little smaller and slimmer than Peregrine. Upperside dark grey-brown with paler fringes. Cheek white, crown grey with rufous patch at hind-crown. Cheek white with narrow dark moustachial stripe. Underside white with black spotting, forming bars on flanks. Juvenile browner; underside washed buff and marked with heavy dark streaks. Shows strongly, evenly barred flight feathers and tail in flight. Gives harsh, rasping calls. Mainly hunts birds, catching them in air after stoop or short chase. Prefers open, arid countryside. Nests on cliff ledge or in old birds' nest in tree. Widespread though rather uncommon; absent in north and on Sardinia.

PEREGRINE FALCON *Falco peregrinus* 42cm

A large falcon; powerful and stocky. Adult dark slate-grey above, white below with black barring. Dark crown and broad dark moustachial stripe stand out against white cheek. Underwings finely barred. Juvenile browner, underparts buff-tinted and marked with heavy dark vertical streaks. Looks broad-winged in flight; rump pale and silvery-blue. Call a loud, harsh and whining *kreeh kreeh*, very vocal near nest. Hunts birds on wing, stooping from height to strike prey. Nests on cliff ledge, sometimes on high buildings. Hunts over open countryside, especially coastal; attracted to gatherings of waders and wildfowl. Fairly common widespread resident.

▼ *Adult*   ▼ *Juvenile*

ROSE-RINGED PARAKEET
Psittacula krameri **40cm**

Brilliant green, very long-tailed parrot, native to Asia and Africa. Male has black chin and narrow black collar with pink edge at nape; female and juvenile have no black. Eye-ring and bill red, feet grey. In flight shows darker flight feathers than inner wing. Blue and yellow forms occasionally seen. Call a loud harsh screech; travelling flocks are very noisy. Feeds on plant buds, fruit and seeds. Mainly forages high in tree canopy, climbing nimbly among branches; holds food with foot while eating. Gregarious outside breeding season. Nests in tree-holes. Feral birds established mainly in city parks, including Rome. Localised resident.

GOLDEN ORIOLE *Oriolus oriolus* **23cm**

Colourful but surprisingly hard-to-see bird. Robust shape, recalling miniature crow. Male bright yellow with black tail, wings and lores, yellow patch midway down folded wing, and yellow tail corners. Female drabber, yellow-green with darker wings; grey-white below with darker streaks; juvenile greyer and more uniform. Eye and bill dark pink, legs grey. Song a loud, exotic-sounding fluty whistle; also has harsh crow-like calls. Forages and nests in high treetops, where it is well camouflaged among foliage. Found in mature deciduous woodland, often near watercourses, also in large parks and gardens. A fairly widespread summer visitor.

▼ *Adult male*

▼ *Adult female*

 ▲ Adult male   ▲ Adult female

RED-BACKED SHRIKE *Lanius collurio* 17cm

A fairly small shrike with typical large-headed, long-tailed shape. Male has grey cap and black eye-mask, chestnut back and wings, dark tail and white underside with rosy flush. In flight shows distinctive tail pattern – broad black terminal band and central stripe, sides white. Female and juvenile like very drab, grey-brown male, with dark scaly pattern on underside. Calls short, harsh notes, song quiet, warbler-like with mimicry. Hunts large insects, sometimes impaling them on thorns to store. Watches for prey from prominent perch. Found in open scrubby countryside; farmland, orchards, olive groves, vineyards. Common and widespread summer visitor.

LESSER GREY SHRIKE *Lanius minor* 20cm

More compact, less variegated than Great Grey Shrike. Adult has grey crown and black mask (reaching forehead) with no white between. Back grey, wings black, underparts white with strong peach or rosy flush on breast and belly. In flight shows large white wing patch and white tail-sides. Juvenile like adult but with white scaling on upperparts, only slight peach flush on underside. Quiet but has various harsh, abrupt calls. A typical shrike in its behaviour. Often seen perched on overhead wires, looking for prey. Found in fairly open but well-vegetated habitats with bushes and scattered trees; cultivated land. Scarce, local and declining summer visitor; not on Sardinia.

▲ Adult female   ▲ Adult male

WOODCHAT SHRIKE *Lanius senator* 18cm

Stocky, boldly marked shrike. Male has chestnut crown, black face mask. Wings black with white patches, tail black, rump white. Underparts white, flushed light buff. Female has faint scaly barring on flanks, markings less clean-cut than male's. In flight shows white sides to back, white comma marking at wing-bend, and white rump, tail sides and tail-tip. Juvenile light grey-brown with darker scaly markings. Song loud, warbler-like with squeaks, grating notes and mimicry, calls short, harsh. Typical shrike behaviour. Often seen perched atop bushes. Habitat varied; open countryside with some trees, some bare ground. Scarce, local and declining summer visitor, commoner in south and on Sardinia.

GREAT GREY SHRIKE *Lanius excubitor* 23cm

The largest shrike. Stocky and long-tailed. Often looks very white. Crown, back and rump grey, wings and tail black. Has narrower black eye-mask than Lesser Grey, with narrow white stripe above eye. Underparts white with faint grey wash on flanks. In flight shows small white wing patch; broad white tail-sides. In juvenile, black areas duller, greyer; shows thin white wing-bar. Call a soft trill. A formidable predator, killing small birds and other vertebrates as well as insects; impales prey for later consumption. Has bounding flight, interrupted with short hovers. Prefers remote open countryside; boggy fields with scrub, moorland, heaths. A scarce winter visitor to northern and central Italy.

CHOUGH *Pyrrhocorax pyrrhocorax* 39cm

A small, graceful, all-black crow with a long, down-curved bill and pink legs. Adult is glossy black, with red bill, juvenile dull black with shorter, yellow bill. In flight shows broad wings with very long 'fingered' primary feather tips; underwing shows dark inner wing contrasting with more translucent flight feathers. Call a rather piercing, harsh, whirring *chiahh*. Very agile and aerobatic in flight. Gregarious, usually seen in family groups or larger parties. Feeds on ground, probing for worms. Nests on rocky ledge, sometimes on buildings. Prefers open, rugged upland habitats with cliff faces. Resident in western Alps and Apennines, very rare and localised elsewhere (Sardinia and Sicily).

ALPINE CHOUGH *Pyrrhocorax graculus* 37cm

Smaller and shorter-billed than Chough, with shorter legs but longer tail. Adult and juvenile both have yellow bills, with barely noticeable down-curve. In flight tail base looks 'pinched in', wings less deeply 'fingered' than in Chough. Usual call very different to Chough's, a high buzzing *zihhhr*. Gregarious, often in very large flocks which fly in compact formation, dipping, diving and rising in unison. Feeds on ground on invertebrates in summer, switching to plant matter in winter; also scavenges around ski lodges and other habitation. A bird of high mountains (above *c.*1,500 metres), nesting on rocky ledges. Resident in Alps and Apennines.

JAY *Garrulus glandarius* 33cm

A colourful small crow. Body plumage mainly pinkish-peach, darker and greyer on back. Wing black and white, with patch of bright blue, black-barred feathers at wing-bend. Tail black, rump white. Black stripe below cheek, fine black streaks on crown. Eye pale, bill black, legs pinkish. Round-winged in flight, very direct with steady wingbeats, white rump prominent. Usual call a harsh screech; sometimes imitates various birds of prey. A woodland bird, often very shy and quick to startle. Omnivorous, taking insects, eggs and nestlings in summer, and storing large numbers of acorns in autumn. Common, widespread resident.

MAGPIE *Pica pica* 45cm

Unmistakeable, very long-tailed black-and-white crow with longish legs. Plumage black, glossed green and violet, with white belly (not reaching legs) and large white patch in wing. In flight broad-winged, shows white outer flight feathers with black edges; graduated tail shape. Juvenile like adult but shorter tail when newly fledged. Calls are various rattling cackles and harsh or whining squawks. Takes varied diet, searching for food on ground with strutting walk or powerful hops. Scavenges carrion, raids birds' nests. Loudly mobs predators such as foxes. Often seen in small groups. Nests in trees, found in all kinds of lowland habitats. A common, widespread resident.

▲ Adult in flight   ▲ Adult

NUTCRACKER *Nucifraga caryocatactes* 33cm

Distinctive small crow with front-heavy proportions; short tail, long, heavy bill. Plumage brown with dense large white spots, wings and crown uniform dark brown. Undertail and tail-tip white. Eye dark. Round-winged in flight, white tail markings conspicuous. Quiet, but sometimes gives a rattling *krrrrrr* call. A specialist feeder on pine seeds, opening cones by gripping with foot while probing and prising cone open with its bill; also eats other seeds. Takes insects and other animal prey in spring and summer. Found in upland coniferous forest. In Italy restricted to Alps, where common resident, but occasionally 'irrupts' further south in winter.

JACKDAW *Corvus monedula* 32cm

Compact small, black crow. Adult has silvery-grey neck cowl, contrasting with black face, otherwise rather matte black. Juvenile completely black. Eye white (blue in juvenile), bill small and thick, black. Looks blunt-headed in flight relative to larger, longer-billed crows; has fast agile flight. Usual call a loud, bright, chuckling *tchack*, also downslurred *kyarrh*. Gregarious, often seen flying in large numbers, with pairs sticking close together within flock. Feeds mainly on ground, forages in farmland and other open habitats, omnivorous. Nests on rocky ledges, on buildings or in hollow trees, singly or in colonies. Common, widespread resident.

ROOK *Corvus frugilegus* 45cm

A largish, rangy, loose-plumaged black crow with longish straight bill. Has shaggy 'trousers' and a peaked crown; particularly striking in adult birds. Plumage has blue gloss. Adult has bare, crusty white bill base reaching to eyes; juvenile fully feathered on face and best told from Carrion Crow by head shape and straightness of bill. In flight shows deeply 'fingered' wingtips and round-ended tail. Calls various harsh, baleful-sounding caws. Gregarious, feeding in flocks and nesting in colonies (rookeries) in treetops. Will join foraging flocks of Jackdaws. Found on farmland with some mature trees. Feeds on worms, insects and plant material. Winter visitor to northern Italy.

RAVEN *Corvus corax* 60cm

The largest crow. All-black, with powerful build, very strong bill with marked downward curve on upper mandible, head looks small relative to bill. Throat feathers often have puffed-out, shaggy appearance. In flight shows diamond-shaped tail. Very agile and aerobatic, performing spectacular tumbles and turns. Voice a deep, resonant, rolling croak. Often seen in pairs patrolling territory, will chase birds of prey. Omnivorous, very attracted to carrion, can also kill quite large prey (such as rabbits). Nests on a rocky crag or in a tree; nest very large. Most common in more remote upland areas. A localised resident.

CARRION CROW *Corvus corone* 48cm

Largish all-black crow, the northern counterpart of Hooded Crow and very like it in all respects except plumage. Smaller and more compact than Raven; sleeker than Rook with more rounded head and more curved upper mandible to bill. In flight less agile than smaller Jackdaw or larger Raven; flies in direct line with steady 'rowing' wingbeats. Calls very varied, ranging from a generic mid-pitched caw, often given in series, to higher squeaking or ringing notes. An adaptable omnivore; will scavenge carrion, forage along strandline and at rubbish dumps. A common resident in Alps, and hybridises readily with Hooded Crow.

HOODED CROW *Corvus cornix* 48cm

A largish black-and-grey crow, not readily confusable with any other species. Body plumage dull grey-brown; head, wings and tail black. Black from head spreads down into flaring patch on breast. May hybridise with Carrion Crow; hybrids show more extensive black. Bill black, sturdy, legs dark. Voice as Carrion Crow. Has direct flight with deep wingbeats, not tending towards aerobatics. Not especially gregarious, though groups may gather at rich food supplies. Forages on ground for worms and insects, comes to carrion, visits refuse dumps. Usually shy and wary. Builds large stick nest well-hidden in tree. A common resident throughout Italy.

ALPINE ACCENTOR *Prunella collaris* 16cm

A dark, colourful songbird. Head grey, upperparts grey-brown streaked black with two thin white wing-bars either side of blackish wing panel. Underparts grey shading to rich red-brown. Patch of black-and-white barring on throat. Bill shortish, dark with yellow base. Call is a rolling *drrru* or hard *chak*; song (given by both sexes) is varied, combining trills and squeaky notes. Often seen in small groups; has complex mating system, both sexes forming multiple pairings. Found in sparsely vegetated high uplands; may move to lower ground in winter. Feeds on insects and berries. Resident in Alps and Apennines, more widespread in winter, even along rocky coasts.

DUNNOCK *Prunella modularis* 14cm

Small, inconspicuous, dark songbird. Head and upper breast dull grey with browner cheeks, body brown with dark streaks on back and belly. Female usually has browner, streakier head than male; juvenile spotted on head and breast. Song a short, high-pitched warbled phrase. Call a loud and slightly plaintive single whistle. Feeds mainly on ground, constantly flicking wings and tail. Complex breeding system; much competitive courtship activity in spring. Usually sings from high perch. Takes insects in summer, seeds and berries in winter. A common resident on mountains, in open woodlands with clearings, hedgerows, moorlands and heaths; more widespread in winter in open, scrubby areas.

▽ *Adult breeding*

▽ *Juvenile*

▲ *Adult male*　　　　　　　　　▲ *Adult female*

HOUSE SPARROW *Passer domesticus* 15cm

The most common sparrow in much of Europe, though not in Italy. Male grey on underside, streaky brown above, with black chin and bib (largest in spring/summer), dark lores, grey crown bordered with brown. Female similar but with plainer head, lacking black markings, pale supercilium. Calls are various loud chirps and chatters. Very social, foraging and resting in groups, often with other seed-eating birds, and nesting in loose colonies. Frequently dust-bathes. Found in urban environments and around farms, visiting grain stores and harvested crop fields, takes more insects. In Italy resident found only in far north; elsewhere replaced by Italian Sparrow.

ITALIAN SPARROW *Passer italiae* 15cm

Very closely related to House Sparrow; females of the two species are indistinguishable. Male Italian Sparrow like male House Sparrow but has entirely chestnut-brown crown and whiter cheeks; black of lores extends behind eye as short eye-stripe. Underside a slightly paler shade of grey. Voice, behaviour and biology as that of House Sparrow. This species was formerly considered to be hybrid between House Sparrow and Spanish Sparrow (the latter a common bird in southern Europe, both east and west of Italy) but is now treated as full species. A common resident of mainland Italy and Sicily.

▼ *Adult male breeding*　　　　▼ *Adult female*

▲ *Adult male*   ▲ *Adult female*

SPANISH SPARROW *Passer hispaniolensis* 15cm

Closely related to House and Italian Sparrows; females usually indistinguishable though may show hint of dark grey streaking on flanks. Male distinctive and very boldly patterned in black, chestnut and whitish, in summer particularly almost lacks dull grey tones of other species. Crown chestnut, has narrow white supercilium and black eye-stripe. Black bib spreads as heavy streaking down breast, onto flanks and sides of undertail, also on back. Wings chestnut with double white wing-bar. In winter pattern more subdued. Voice and habits similar to House and Italian Sparrows, may prefer more rural habitats. Resident on Sardinia, and parts of Sicily and south-east mainland Italy.

TREE SPARROW *Passer montanus* 13cm

The smallest sparrow and the only one in which the sexes are identical. Boldly and neatly marked. Crown chestnut, neck-sides and cheek white, with black spot below eye. Small black bib. Underside light grey-brown, upperside streaky chestnut with narrow double white wing-bar. Juvenile more muted but has same face pattern. Has chirping calls, also distinctive bright two-note *ts-wit*. Feeds on insects and seeds; gregarious. More rural than other sparrows but still often found around habitation; in villages and small towns, and on farmland. Will flock with other small seed-eaters. A common and widespread resident, including on Sardinia and Sicily.

WHITE-WINGED SNOWFINCH *Montifringilla nivalis* 17cm

A relatively large and distinctive sparrow-like bird of mountainous regions. Rather slim and long-bodied, with long tail. White on underparts, tail-sides and most of wings; head grey, back grey-brown with faint darker streaks. In breeding plumage has black bib and black bill (dull yellow in winter). In flight shows bold pattern of white, black-tipped wings, and black, white-edged tail. Has varied calls including mewing, chattering and rolling notes; song a jerky twittering. A bird of high altitudes, rarely seen below 1,500 metres; often forages around ski lodges and can be very approachable. Resident in Alps and Apennines.

TREE PIPIT *Anthus trivialis* 15cm

A light-coloured, neatly patterned pipit. Upperparts light brown with black streaks, underparts whitish-buff with black streaks on breast, which thin out to fine 'pencil lines' on flanks. Has well-marked face with slight dark eye-stripe and pale supercilium. Legs pinkish, hindclaw shorter than in Meadow Pipit. Bill somewhat stout for a pipit, with pink base. Song a long phrase of varied trills, often given in parachuting song-flight from treetop to ground level; legs dangle as it descends. Call a slightly hoarse *spizzz*. Prefers mountain woodland edges, or more open country with some tall trees. A fairly widespread summer visitor and passage migrant.

MEADOW PIPIT *Anthus pratensis* 15cm

(Near Threatened) Very like Tree Pipit. Has less well-marked face, giving gentler expression. Streaking on flanks is same thickness as on breast. Breast streaking sometimes coalesces to form solid dark patch. Legs pinkish; strikingly elongated hind claw. Call a sweet, slightly plaintive *weet weet weet*, given when flushed from ground vegetation. Song a series of repeated notes, often given in rising song-flight that begins and ends at ground level. Forages mostly on ground, walking or running in pursuit of insect prey; somewhat gregarious. Found in open countryside – grassland, farmland, moor and heath. A widespread winter visitor to Italy.

WATER PIPIT *Anthus spinoletta* 16cm

A robust pipit, larger than Meadow and Tree Pipits. In breeding plumage rather plain grey on crown, cheeks and back; wings dark with bold pale feather fringes. Has strong white supercilium. Underparts whitish, with hint of darker streaking on flanks and variable (sometimes very strong) pink flush to chin and breast. Legs dark. In winter loses pink tint and underparts marked with strong streaks on breast and flanks. Song protracted, varied trilling, call a sharp *pssit*. Breeds on high-altitude bare slopes and fields, and moves to marshy lowlands in winter. A localised summer visitor to mountainous regions, and much more widespread in winter.

▽ *Adult breeding*   ▽ *Adult non-breeding*

TAWNY PIPIT   *Anthus campestris*   17cm

A large, pale, wagtail-like pipit. Very slim and long-legged. Pale grey-brown fading to almost white on breast and belly. Wing feathers dark-centred with pale fringes. Hint of darker streaking on back and breast-sides. Face well-marked with dark eye-stripe, pale supercilium, dark stripe below eye and another stretching down from bill base. Juvenile darker, with dark scalloping on back and streaks on breast. Call a sparrow-like chirrup, song a repeated two- or three-note phrase. Has strutting walk, searching on ground for insect prey. Found on sparsely vegetated dry, open, flat ground in highlands and lowlands. A fairly common summer visitor.

YELLOW WAGTAIL   *Motacilla flava cinereocapilla*   15cm

Smallish wagtail. Many subspecies in Europe, differing in male's head colours and pattern. Subspecies *cinereocapilla* (Ashy-headed Wagtail) breeds commonly in Italy. Male has dark grey head, blackish cheeks and white chin, otherwise olive green above and bright yellow below. Female more muted, with light grey head and pale supercilium. Has white outer tail-feathers and narrow double white wing-bars; legs black. Subspecies *feldegg* (Black-headed) is a regular but scarce and localised breeder, mainly in south. Call a high *tsit*, song a simple short phrase of dry notes. Prefers damp lowland grassland and marshes. Often associates with large livestock. A fairly widespread summer visitor and passage migrant; other subspecies regular on migration.

◀ *From top: adult male* cinereocapilla, *adult male* feldegg, *adult male* flava

GREY WAGTAIL *Motacilla cinerea* 19cm

Largish wagtail with very long tail. Upperside plain blue-grey, underside yellow (brightest under tail). Lacks white wing-bars but tertial feathers have white fringes. Has narrow white supercilium and white outer tail feathers; breeding-plumaged male has black throat. Female may have dusky or white throat. Juvenile has yellow restricted to undertail; breast pale with slight pinkish tint. Legs greyish-pink. Call a sharp two-note *chi-tick*; song short phrase of hissing notes. Very active, constantly bobbing tail, makes dashing flights to catch flies over water. Most often seen near fast-flowing, rocky streams and rivers, in winter also on lake shores, sometimes in towns. A common, widespread resident.

▲ *Adult male breeding*
▼ *Adult non-breeding*

WHITE WAGTAIL *Motacilla alba* 17cm

Dapper black, white and grey wagtail. Back grey, underside white, wings grey with darker feather centres and double white wing-bar. In breeding plumage, head white with black hind-crown and neck, large black bib; male a little more crisply marked than female. In winter, throat white, crown grey, bib reduced to black breast-band. Juvenile duskier with yellow tint on face. Legs black. Call a shrill *chissick*, song a simple twitter. Has sprightly gait, tail constantly bobbing, sprints to catch insect prey. Found in open countryside, often near flowing or still water and/or close to human habitation. A common, widespread resident.

▲ *Adult non-breeding*
▼ *Adult breeding*

▲ Adult male breeding ▲ Adult female

CHAFFINCH *Fringilla coelebs* 15cm

A sparrow-sized finch. Male colourful, with soft pink cheeks and underparts, maroon back, blue-grey crown, and black wings with white shoulder and white wing-bar that forms a 'T' shape. Rump greenish, tail dark with white outer feathers. Generally duller in winter. Female has similar wing and tail pattern, but body plumage drab grey-brown, no strong facial markings. Call a bright *twink* or more mournful *dwee*, song a fast, descending chirruped phrase. Feeds on insects in summer, seeds in winter. Gregarious when not breeding, will flock with other seed-eaters. Often forages on the ground. A bird of open woodlands, gardens and parkland. Common, widespread resident.

BRAMBLING *Fringilla montifringilla* 15cm

The northerly counterpart of Chaffinch. Similar in general shape and pattern, but breast orange rather than pink, shading to white on belly with black spots on flanks; shoulder patch orange. Head grey with dark crown and neck-sides; male also has blackish markings around eye which become more extensive as spring approaches. Black tail, white rump. Call a harsh two-note *te-chup*. Sociable and often joins flocks of Chaffinches; feeds on seed, with particular liking for beech mast. A winter visitor to Italy; may be seen anywhere in the country although numbers vary year on year (sometimes abundant); more likely in north and in mountains.

▼ Adult male winter ▼ Adult female winter

HAWFINCH *Coccothraustes coccothraustes* 17cm

Big, stocky finch. Short tail and very large head and bill give unique outline. Mainly pinkish-orange, with dark back, whitish shoulder patch and blue-grey on flight feathers. Head orange, neck grey, has small black bib and black lores. Bill blue-grey. Tail has broad white tip. Female slightly drabber than male. Call a hard, buzzing or grating *tsick*, song a quiet series of similar notes. A shy bird, tending to keep to the high treetops. Found in undisturbed mixed woodland, particularly with some fruit trees (fond of cherries and able to crack their stones). Patchily distributed resident in hills and mountains, in winter may visit grasslands and towns.

BULLFINCH *Pyrrhula pyrrhula* 16cm

Stocky finch with short but very stout bill. Male has bright pink cheeks and underparts, black cap and small black bib, ash-grey back, black wings with white wing-bar, white rump and black tail. Female has the same pattern but colours much more muted; underparts soft pinkish-grey. Juvenile much browner and lacks black head markings. Call a soft, hesitant single whistle. Song quiet, combines melodious fluting notes with squeaks and rattles. Usually seen in pairs or small groups, shy and inconspicuous as it feeds in trees or shrubs. Breeds in woodland, parks, larger gardens in Alps and Apennines. A fairly widespread resident, wandering more widely in winter.

▲ Adult male　　　▲ Adult female

GREENFINCH *Chloris chloris* 15cm

Stout, large-billed and large-headed finch. Male quite uniform mossy green, with hints of grey on cheeks, flanks and wings; some look very yellow. Has dark flight feathers and yellow along wing edge and tail-sides. Bill rather pale. Female similar but greyer; juvenile strongly streaked on both upperparts and underparts. Call a rather metallic chirping note. Song varied, with fast twitters and drawn-out downslurred notes, sometimes given in circling, butterfly-like song-flight. Feeds on ground and in trees. Often gregarious in winter, may be aggressive to other finches. Found in woodland, hedgerows, gardens and parks. A common, widespread resident.

LINNET *Linaria cannabina* 13cm

Smallish, long-tailed finch. Male has grey head with red forehead patch, unmarked chestnut-brown back, and pale underparts with pink flush on breast, strongest in summer. Female is duller brown with light streaks on back and breast; juvenile is more heavily streaked. Bill and legs grey. All plumages have white panel along wing edge. Call a bright buzzy *tit-it*, song a pleasant series of twittered phrases. Forms large flocks in winter, which visit weedy fields to eat seeds. Prefers open countryside – farmland, meadows with hedgerows, usually on hills or mountains but also down to sea-level in south Italy. A fairly common and widespread resident.

▼ Adult male　　　▼ Adult female

COMMON REDPOLL *Acanthis flammea* 12cm

A very small, agile, fork-tailed finch. Plumage light grey-brown with darker streaks on upperside and underside. Has broad pale wing-bar. Head distinctive with small red forehead patch, black lores and small black bib, short black eye-stripe. Breast flushed reddish-pink in adult males; females and younger birds have little or no pink. Bill yellow with black tip. Call a hard *tet tet*. Found in woodland, parks and gardens. Feeds mainly in high treetops, extracting seeds from alder cones or similar, often dangling upside-down. Usually in flocks, sometimes with Siskins. A rather common resident in Alps; some birds stray to northern plains in winter.

COMMON CROSSBILL *Loxia curvirostra* 16cm

A robust, short-tailed finch with a unique bill shape, the mandible tips elongated and crossing over. Male is rich red, almost unmarked, with darker wings and tail. Female similarly patterned but in mossy green, with yellowish rump. Juvenile rather grey, and heavily streaked all over. Call a distinctive metallic *klip*. A specialist feeder on pine cones, which it grips in its foot while prising the scales apart with its bill to access the seed. Usually in small flocks. Found in coniferous forest, or smaller stands of pines in more open countryside. Localised resident, but inclined to periodic irruptive movements when it may be seen almost anywhere.

▼ *Adult male*　　　　　　　　▼ *Adult female*

GOLDFINCH *Carduelis carduelis* 13cm

Distinctive, colourful slim finch. Sexes alike. Body plumage light brown, shading to white on belly. Face white with red mask around bill base, and black crown and cheek-sides. Wings black with bold yellow wing-bar and white spots in wingtip; rump white, tail black with white spots at tip. Juvenile streaked light brown with adult-like wings and tail. Bill slimmish, pale with dark tip. Call a cheerful, laughing twitter, song extended series of similar notes. Breeds at woodland edges, hedgerows, parks and gardens. Semi-colonial nester and highly gregarious in autumn and winter, flocks visiting weedy meadows with thistles. Common, widespread resident.

CORSICAN FINCH *Carduelis corsicana* 12cm

Small slim finch. Front of face, rump and entire underparts bright yellow, back of neck grey, back brown with darker streaks, wings black with broad, double wing-bars and feather edges in yellow-green. Bill dark. Female a little drabber than male. Calls are short *te* or *teh* notes; song a series of trills of varying speed. A close relative of more northerly Citril Finch (see photo below) and formerly considered a subspecies of it; found only on Corsica, Sardinia, Elba, Capraia and Gorgona Islands. Found in scrubby heathland and forest edges, from sea-level to the mountains; tends to forage on ground. Feeds on seeds and insects. Resident.

▼ *Corsican Finch*

▼ *Citril Finch*

▲ *Adult male*　　　　　　　▲ *Adult female*

SERIN *Serinus serinus* 11cm

Tiny, short-billed finch. Male has bright yellow face and breast, fading to white on belly; flanks marked with bold dark streaks. Upperparts green with black streaks on flanks and breast-sides, wings and tail blackish, showing yellow rump and tail-sides in flight. Female similar but yellow areas replaced with duller yellow-green. Juvenile browner, heavily streaked. Call a high-pitched buzzing trill; song similar with shivering, electrical quality. Feeds on ground and in treetops, taking seeds and insects. Usually alone or in pairs, in light woodland, parks and gardens. A common and widespread resident; summer visitor only in the far north.

SISKIN *Spinus spinus* 12cm

Small green finch with rather long, pointed bill. Male boldly marked with yellow face, breast, wing-bars, tail-sides and rump; crown, bib and most of wings blackish, back green with fine dark streaks; belly white with dark streaks on flanks. Female has less yellow, and lacks black face markings. Juvenile greyer, heavily streaked. Has nasal two-note *dzwee* or *dzee-oo* call. Song a long series of varied, high-pitched trills. In winter travels in flocks, sometimes with Common Redpolls, and feeds in high treetops on various tree seeds, also on ground at times. Prefers coniferous or mixed woodland. Very agile, tit-like in its actions. Localised resident, widespread in winter.

▼ *Adult male*　　　　　　　▼ *Adult female*

▲ Adult male breeding ▲ Adult female

BLACK-HEADED BUNTING *Emberiza melanocephala* 16cm

A large, colourful bunting. Male has black head, bright yellow chin, collar and underside, and chestnut back. Wings dark with broad pale feather fringes and tips, creating double white wing-bars. Female similar but has grey head shading to grey-brown back, no collar. Juvenile much greyer, with just a little yellow on throat and belly. Has various brief, dry calls; song is simple dry, rattling trill. A bird of open countryside with scrub, scattered trees or hedgerows; male sings from the top of a bush or a wire. Often forages on the ground. Summer visitor to south-east Italy, a few small colonies elsewhere; not Sicily or Sardinia.

CORN BUNTING *Emberiza calandra* 18cm

Large, stocky, long-tailed bunting with very plain plumage. Light earth-brown on upperparts, a shade paler below, marked with broad darker streaks on crown, back and shoulders; fine streaks on underparts. Face rather plain but with pale stripe outlining cheek, fine dark stripe below. Bill stout, grey at tip, pinkish at base. Often dangles legs in flight. Call is hard, metallic *tsriiit*, song a short rattle likened to a bunch of keys being shaken. Found in open countryside, particularly farmland, and nests at ground level; male uses bush, fencepost or overhead wire as song perch. Common, widespread resident.

ROCK BUNTING *Emberiza cia* 16cm

Slim, medium-sized bunting. Grey head and breast, rest of plumage reddish-brown. Head well-marked with black eye-stripe, also black stripes on crown-sides and outlining cheek. Back has heavy dark streaking, wing-feathers dark-centred and pale-tipped to form double white wing-bar. Underside unmarked. Call a sharp *tsi* or more drawn-out *tsiiu*, song sweet, clear and melodic. Prefers open, rugged and rocky countryside, primarily in uplands, with sparse scrubby vegetation. Can be quite tame and confiding, though unobtrusive as it feeds quietly on ground. Resident in montane regions, and becomes more widespread in winter as some move to lower ground.

ORTOLAN BUNTING *Emberiza hortulana* 16cm

Slim, long-tailed bunting. Head and breast soft grey-green, with yellowish throat and cheek-stripe; yellow eye-ring strongly accentuates dark eye. Underparts unmarked orange-brown. Upperparts grey-brown; wing-feathers have dark centres and pale fringes. Young birds have some spotting on breast and flanks. Bill and legs pinkish. Has various brief, metallic calls, and a clear but simple ringing song of evenly spaced notes, the second half of the phrase slightly softer and lower. A timid inhabitant of woodland edges, farmland with patches of woodland, and similar habitats on dry hills and mountains. Scarce and declining summer visitor mainly to northern and central Italy, passage migrant in south.

▲ Adult male ▲ Adult female

CIRL BUNTING *Emberiza cirlus* 16cm

Male is colourful bunting with yellow on face and yellow belly, with dark green crown, collar and breast-band, and black throat and eye-stripe. Flanks streaked rusty-brown. Upperside greenish-brown, with streaked back and wings. Female much drabber, lacking black head-markings, more streaked on underparts; best told from female Yellowhammer by grey-green rather than chestnut-brown rump. Juvenile whitish on belly with heavy streaking. Call a hard *zit*; song a simple dry rattle recalling Lesser Whitethroat. Found on farmland with hedgerows, vineyards, large gardens, in both upland and lowland countryside, up to about 1,500 metres. Common, widespread resident.

YELLOWHAMMER *Emberiza citrinella* 16cm

A close relative of Cirl Bunting. Male has yellow head and underparts, with narrow dark eye-stripe, cheek-stripe and crown streaks (some have solid yellow head). Breast-sides rusty chestnut, extending in streaks along flanks. Upperparts light grey-brown, with darker streaks. Rump reddish-brown. Female and juvenile much drabber and streakier, though still with yellowish overall look. Has dry, brief calls. Song a short rattle with drawn-out final note. Found on farmland with hedgerows, and similar open countryside with some scrub, on hills and mountains. A common resident over much of Italy (scarce in south), more widespread in winter down to sea-level. Not on Sardinia.

▲ Adult male

▲ Adult female

REED BUNTING *Emberiza schoeniclus* 14cm

Rather small, sparrow-like bunting. Male in breeding plumage has black head and breast, with white collar and cheek-stripe; almost unmarked pale underparts. Upperparts dark brown, streaked with black. Outer tail-feathers white. Female has brown rather than black head, with pale chin and supercilium, grey rather than white collar, underside strongly streaked. Has short, buzzy calls, and simple song comprising two distinct notes followed by a short jangling phrase. Mainly found in wetland areas with reedbeds, though may move to farmland in winter. Rather localised resident, more widespread in winter; birds from migratory populations further north and east pass through.

COAL TIT *Periparus ater* 11cm

Small, large-headed tit. Has black cap and large flared black bib, white cheeks and white stripe on nape. Upperparts grey with double white wing-bar; underparts buffish-grey. When crown feathers are raised, it shows a small pointed crest. Juvenile duller, tinted yellowish. Has ringing single-note calls, and song is usually a fast, repeated two-note phrase. A typical very active tit, feeding mainly in treetops and often hovering or dangling from thin twigs. Will form loose flocks in winter, sometimes with other tits and woodland birds. Mainly found in pine forest. Fairly widespread resident, mostly found in upland parts of mainland interior.

CRESTED TIT *Lophophanes cristatus* 11cm

Small tit with pointed crest. Upperparts warm mid-brown, underparts paler with buff wash. Head white, with black throat and narrow black stripe encircling neck; also has dark eye-stripe joining curved cheek-stripe behind eye. Crest marked with fine black-and-white barring, comes to tall point above centre of crown when bird is excited; otherwise held more flattened. Eye dark red. Call a very high-pitched bubbly, cheerful trill; song combines trills and short, sharp notes. Found in woodland (especially coniferous), where it feeds mainly in high treetops, picking insect prey from fine twigs. Flocks with other tits in winter. Resident in Alps and north Apennines (increasing).

WILLOW TIT *Poecile montanus* 12cm

A big-headed, black-capped tit. Upperparts light grey-brown, with faint paler wing panel. Underparts white, shading to buff on flanks and undertail. Cheeks whitish, cap black, has small black bib. Very like Marsh Tit; best separated by call, a repeated drawn-out nasal *djerrrr*. Song a series of sweet, rather slow notes; also a faster trill. Found mainly in pine forest in upland, hilly countryside. Feeds at all levels in trees, and excavates nesting hole in soft decaying wood rather than using old woodpecker hole or other existing cavity. A localised resident in Alps and Apennines.

MARSH TIT *Poecile palustris* 12cm

Like Willow Tit in general appearance. Best distinguished by call, but also a few subtle features (often easier to see in photographs). Has white spot at base of upper mandible (Willow has all-black bill); and cheek is neatly two-toned with dividing line between white at front of face and light grey-brown wash behind. Lacks wing-panel. Shape slightly different – more balanced proportions compared to somewhat big-headed, thick-necked and 'egg-shaped' Willow. Call a sneezing *pit-choo*; song a repeated single- or two-note phrase. Found in deciduous woodland (not marshes!) and sometimes parks and gardens. Typical tit behaviour. Widespread, fairly common resident, not on Sardinia.

BLUE TIT *Cyanistes caeruleus* 11cm

Colourful small tit. Underparts yellow with narrow dark belly-stripe. Greenish back, shading to blue on wings and tail; narrow white wing-bar. Face white with blue crown patch outlined in white, dark bib, dark eye-stripe and cheek-stripe meeting on nape. Juvenile duller, with yellowish cheeks. Call a ringing three-note phrase, last note lower and longer; also churring alarm call. Song similar to call but more extended, last note a trill. Active, agile bird that primarily feeds in treetops. Joins mixed tit flocks in winter. Found in woodland, parks, gardens and other habitats with some trees; will feed in reedbeds in winter. Very common, widespread resident.

GREAT TIT *Parus major* 14cm

Largest tit species; colourful. Head black, cheeks white. Underside yellow with broad black stripe from chin to belly (narrower and petering out at belly in female, wider and broadening at belly in male). Back green, wings and tail bluish, narrow white wing-bar. Juvenile duller all over, with yellowish cheeks. Very varied calls including bright Chaffinch-like *twink* and various more grating notes. Song a repeated two-note phrase, recalling a squeaky gate. Found in woodlands, parks and gardens. Feeds at all levels in trees, taking insects, berries and seeds. Dominates other tit species in mixed feeding flocks. A very common, widespread resident.

PENDULINE TIT *Remiz pendulinus* 11cm

Very small tit-like bird with shortish tail. Head light grey with black eye-mask (more extensive in male). Back red-brown, underparts light peach, with some red-brown spotting on breast forming upper breast-band in male. Wings well-marked with dark feather centres and pale fringes, likewise tail. Juvenile has plain brown head. Bill grey, slim and sharply pointed, legs black. Call a soft downslurred *tsiu*; song includes repeated calls interspersed with high trills. Prefers damp marshy habitats and watercourses with trees; attaches its large, hanging sack-shaped nest to fine twigs; sometimes loosely colonial. Insectivorous. A localised and declining resident, also more widespread passage migrant.

CALANDRA LARK *Melanocorypha calandra* 19cm

A large, stocky, big-billed lark. Light sandy-brown upperparts with darker brown streaking on crown, neck, back and wings. Has pale supercilium and eye-surround, darker cheeks. Black patches on breast-sides, breast otherwise only lightly streaked. In flight shows conspicuous white trailing edge to wing, and solid dark (almost black) underwing. Bill yellowish, darker on top and at tip. Legs short, pink. Call a buzzing dry trill, song a long series of chirping and trilling notes. Singing birds rise to 100 metres or so and 'hang' with slow wingbeats. Open farmland and grassland. Rather uncommon resident in southern Italy (including Sicily and Sardinia).

SHORT-TOED LARK *Calandrella brachydactyla* 15cm

A pale, rather thick-billed lark. Light sandy-coloured on upperside with delicate black streaking, and dark feather centres to wing feathers giving quite strong wing pattern. Underparts almost unmarked white; a little fine streaking on breast-sides. Face pale with sandy cheeks and crown. Bill finch-like; broad-based but sharp-tipped, yellowish. Legs pale pinkish. Can appear slightly crested when crown feathers raised. Call a short dry *trilp*, recalling House Martin; song formed of brief, chirruping phrases, given in undulating song-flight. Prefers dry, sparsely vegetated open habitats, including coastal areas; forages unobtrusively on ground. Patchily distributed uncommon summer visitor, and more widespread passage migrant.

WOODLARK *Lullula arborea* 14cm

Small, short-tailed lark. Well-marked with brown upperparts streaked darker and paler, white underside with buff flush on breast-sides, black streaking on breast. Wing edge has distinctive black-and-white patch at midway point. Pale supercilia, which meet in a downward point on nape. Crown brown streaked black, cheeks unmarked reddish-brown with pale surround. Bill slim, longish, legs pale pink. Shows pale wing-bar and tail-corners in flight; flying outline almost bat-like with broad wings, short tail. Call a fluty, repeated *twe-we*, song melodious, slow and melancholic. Favours dry scrubby habitats; heathland, farmland, also open woodland. A fairly common and widespread resident.

SKYLARK *Alauda arvensis* 17cm

Largish lark, proportionately small-headed, and often shows definite crest. Upperparts light brown with contrasting dark streaks. Underparts pale, washed buff on breast-sides with dark streaking on breast. Has brown crown and cheeks, face otherwise pale. Bill slimmish, legs pink; elongated hind claw. In flight shows pale wing edge. Juvenile has rather scaly look on upperparts; no sign of crest. Call a pleasant dry, rolling *chirrup*. Song protracted series of rapid chirps, whistles and trills, given from towering song-flight. Found in open farmland and grassland, alpine meadows and pasture on mountains, unobtrusive except when singing; forms loose flocks in winter. Common, widespread resident; numbers boosted by migrants in winter.

CRESTED LARK *Galerida cristata* 18cm

A little larger than Skylark, shorter-tailed, with obvious spiky crest. Upperparts mid-brown with darker brown streaks and feather centres. Underparts whitish with dark streaking on breast, becoming finer on flanks. Face plain brown but with dark line down from eye. Bill slim, longish, slightly down-curved. Legs pink, hind claw not elongated. Broad-winged and short-tailed in flight; shows rusty underwing. Call a melancholic two- to four-note whistle. Song very varied, tuneful, given on ground or in flight. Found on dry open habitats including farmland, waste ground, coastal flats, open fields. A fairly common resident in lowland areas.

BEARDED TIT *Panurus biarmicus* 15cm

A unique wetland songbird, resembling tits in shape and behaviour but related to larks. Very long-tailed. Plumage warm orange-brown with contrasting black-and-white patches in wings. Male has grey head with black 'moustache' extending down from base of bill; female has plain brown head. Juvenile more richly orange than adult, with black back, lores and tail-sides. Bill small, yellow (dusky in juvenile female); eyes pale, legs black. Call a dry, metallic *ping*. Song a simple squeaky phrase. Climbs with great agility among reed stems; takes insects in summer, reed seeds in winter. Usually in family groups. A rare, local and declining resident, wandering somewhat in winter.

▼ *Adult female*   ▼ *Adult male*

ZITTING CISTICOLA   *Cisticola juncidis*   10cm

Tiny warbler-like bird with short but broad tail. Light sandy-brown on upperparts, with fine dark streaks on crown, cheeks and rump (crown nearly solid dark in male), and prominent broad dark streaks on back. Underparts unmarked, white with buff wash on breast-sides. Pale eyes, pinkish bill and legs. In flight shows prominent white tail-tip; looks very round-winged. Call *chip*. Male sings in circling, undulating display flight over territory, fanning tail and giving single short, harsh zit calls at regular intervals. Found in mostly lowland grassland with tall grass and some shrubs. A fairly common and widespread resident. Very hard and prolonged winters cause local temporary extinctions.

SAVI'S WARBLER   *Locustella luscinioides*   14cm

Plain, stocky warbler with long, broad, round-ended tail. Upperparts plain warm grey-brown, underparts paler, with whitish throat and centre of belly. Face almost unmarked; slight dark eye-stripe and paler supercilium. Undertail-coverts reach close to tip of tail, giving very thick look to tail base. Legs pinkish. Call a sharp *tzit*; song a continuous dry purring, like a fishing reel being turned. An inconspicuous, skulking bird, usually difficult to observe; climbs through vegetation almost like a small rodent. Found in reedbeds and other dense waterside vegetation. A localised summer visitor to wetlands in northern Italy; may be found elsewhere on migration.

MELODIOUS WARBLER *Hippolais polyglotta* 12cm

A yellow-green warbler with a proportionately large head; looks more robust than *Phylloscopus* warblers. Upperparts unmarked mossy green; underparts yellowish fading to almost white on belly. Face rather plain; dark eye prominent, with yellow eye-ring. Crown often looks peaked. Bill rather strong, with pink base. Legs dull brownish. Has clacking or ticking calls. Song a loud, rapid series of notes, some tuneful, some harsher, somewhat similar to Sedge Warbler; may include some mimicry; often sings in full view. Found in open dry woodland, farmland with hedgerows, vineyards and open habitats with bushes. A common, widespread summer visitor; passage migrant on Sicily and Sardinia.

MOUSTACHED WARBLER *Acrocephalus melanopogon* 13cm

A well-marked, rounded warbler with broad, round-ended tail and short wings. Upperparts warm reddish-brown, with almost black crown and fine black streaks of back and wings. Dark eye-stripe and cheek, white throat and supercilium. Underparts strongly washed reddish-brown, fading to whitish on belly. Legs dark. Call a low *chek*, song a steady, protracted series of repeated *chrr chrr* and similar notes, like Reed Warbler, but includes drawn-out high whistles, recalling Nightingale. Found in reedbeds and other thick waterside vegetation, often feeding close to the water's edge. A scarce and localised resident in a few wetlands in north-west and north-east; more widespread in winter.

SEDGE WARBLER *Acrocephalus schoenobaenus* 12cm

Slightly smaller, slimmer and paler than Moustached Warbler. Mid-brown above with dark streaks, crown darker. Broad creamy supercilium, dark eye-stripe, cheek light brown shading into whitish chin. Underside pale with buff wash on breast-sides. Juvenile has a little streaking on breast-sides. Legs dull pinkish-brown. Gives short sharp calls and low, rolling notes. Song a continuous, excitable series of varied notes; chirrups, squeaks, dry grating sounds, sometimes given in short, steeply rising song-flight. Found in wetlands, including reedbeds but more often slightly drier patches with some scrub. A passage migrant in Italy with a few breeding populations in north-west.

MARSH WARBLER *Acrocephalus palustris* 14cm

Plain-looking wetland warbler, almost identical to Reed Warbler. Dull olive-brown on upperparts, wing feather centres a shade darker. Paler on underside with white throat. Slight pale eye-ring and supercilium in front of eye. Bill relatively heavy with pink base. Legs yellowish-pink. Calls mostly short, quiet notes. Song remarkable – tuneful, varied and including great variety of mimicry of other birds' calls and songs, including African species it encounters in winter. Breeds in thick vegetation in wetland areas, though less tied to reed-beds than Reed Warbler. Skulking and difficult to see. Fairly common summer visitor in north and north-west.

REED WARBLER *Acrocephalus scirpaceus* 13cm

Extremely similar to Marsh Warbler but much more common in Italy. Dull mid-brown on upperparts. Paler on underside with definite white throat. Slight pale eye-ring and supercilium in front of eye. Bill long and slim. Legs dull brownish-pink. Calls soft *che* or *chik*. Song a continuous, steady-paced series of slightly nasal chirruping notes, changing pitch slightly from time to time; sometimes includes mimicry. Forages and breeds in reedbeds; not often seen far from waterside. Often skulking and difficult to see, staying low in reeds, though male sometimes climbs higher while singing. Widespread, common summer visitor.

GREAT REED WARBLER *Acrocephalus arundinaceus* 18cm

Very large warbler; powerful well-proportioned build; as name suggests, it recalls super-sized Reed Warbler. Upperparts mid-brown, underparts paler with white throat and belly, yellow-buff flanks and breast. Dark eye-stripe and narrow pale supercilium. Bill long and heavy, dark with pink base. Eyes mid-brown. Legs greyish, sturdy. Call a throaty *chack*. Song like Reed Warbler's but much louder and stronger, and includes more high-pitched notes. Found in extensive dense reedbeds in marshy areas, sometimes also in smaller stands of reeds alongside waterways. Less skulking than Reed Warbler; often sings in full view. A fairly common and widespread summer visitor.

▲ Adult ▲ Juvenile

HOUSE MARTIN *Delichon urbicum* 14cm

Dapper, black-and-white martin. Upperparts, including upper cheeks, black with blue gloss; has square, white rump patch. Underparts white, including legs (the only songbird with feathered legs and feet). Bill small, dark. Juvenile similar pattern but black less intense and glossy; white areas suffused with tint of dusky grey. Wings broad-based with pointed tips, tail forked. Calls and song are dry rolling twitters. Nests in colonies on buildings (mud cup nest under eaves) or on cliff faces, hunts for flying insect prey over open country and water, often with Barn Swallows and Sand Martins. A common, widespread summer visitor.

BARN SWALLOW *Hirundo rustica* 19cm

Long-tailed, highly aerial bird. Upperparts blackish with bright violet-blue gloss. Has dark orange forehead patch and throat, dark breast-band. Underparts whitish with variable peachy tint. Outer tail feathers narrow, long (especially in male), producing deeply forked shape; tail shows white spots near feather bases when fanned. Juvenile's colours are more muted, and tail shorter, lacking elongated outer tail feathers. Has pleasant twittering calls, and a sharper *vit* note, extended to *si-vit* when alarmed; alerts rest of colony to presence of predator. Nests on ledges inside buildings; hawks for flies over meadows, farmland, open water, often flying very low. Common, widespread summer visitor.

CRAG MARTIN *Ptyonoprogne rupestris* 14cm

A robust, drab martin. Upperparts mid grey-brown. Underparts a shade paler. Has faint dark streaks on throat and mottling on undertail. In flight shows white patches in tail feathers, close to tips, and prominent blackish underwing-coverts. Tail has shallow notch (disappearing when tail fanned). Looks stockier and broader-winged than other martins, though still agile in pursuit of flying insects. Has various short, somewhat nondescript calls; song a quiet rapid twittering. Nests in crevices in cliffs, also in walls of old buildings or under bridges, often in upland areas. In Italy found mainly in montane regions; migrants from further north pass through on passage.

SAND MARTIN *Riparia riparia* 12cm

The smallest martin; looks slim and insubstantial in flight. Upperparts entire warm mid-brown; even in poor light it is easy to tell from House Martin by lack of white rump patch. Underparts whitish, with clear-cut brown breast-band. White throat patch curves up behind cheek, there fading into brown. Tail has shallow fork. Voice very dry, grating; gives short single notes and longer series when at nest. Colonial breeder, excavating tunnels in soft earth banks; often next to water but also in quarries or similar. Mostly hunts over open water. A fairly widespread summer visitor, and very widespread passage migrant.

WESTERN BONELLI'S WARBLER *Phylloscopus bonelli* 11cm

A small, plain-faced leaf warbler. Crown and back dull grey-green, but wings, rump and tail much brighter green (with dark feather centres to wings and tail). Face greyish with full pale eye-ring; dark eye prominent. Shows a hint of dark eye-stripe and paler supercilium. Underside white. Bill shortish and strong-looking with pink base. Legs dull greyish. Call a two-note, upslurred *hu-wee*; song a repeated high-pitched fine note. Prefers dry woodland, mainly oak and pine, on hills and mountains; forages in high treetops, often hovering to pick insects from leaves. A summer visitor mainly to upland areas of central and northern Italy; passage migrant elsewhere.

WOOD WARBLER *Phylloscopus sibilatrix* 12cm

Brightly coloured, rather large leaf warbler with relatively big head, short tail and long wings. Upperparts quite bright mid-green; flight feathers blackish with white fringes. Face, throat and upper breast bright yellow; has dark eye-stripe with yellow supercilium. Belly clean silky white. Legs dull greenish. Call a short *zip*. Song combines very high, shivering trills with series of slower, purer *tyuh* notes. Favours deciduous woodland, where it blends in well with fresh spring foliage; sings and forages in treetops but nests close to or on ground. Summer visitor, most common in central upland areas, passage migrant elsewhere.

WILLOW WARBLER *Phylloscopus trochilus* 12cm

Slimmer and duller than Wood Warbler. Upperparts mossy olive-green, underparts yellow-green, fading to almost white on lower belly. Has dark eye-stripe and pale supercilium, cheeks also rather pale with faint darker outline. Legs usually pinkish. Juvenile rather brighter, with yellow on entire underside. Call a two-note *hoo-weet*. Song (which may be given by birds on migration) a sweet steady series of descending notes, somewhat recalling a slowed-down Chaffinch but without final flourish. Found in woodlands, parks, gardens and other habitats with at least some trees. A northern European summer visitor, occuring as common passage migrant in Italy.

CHIFFCHAFF *Phylloscopus collybita* 11cm

Very like Willow Warbler but a little drabber and less sleek-looking, with shorter wings. Upperparts mossy olive-green, underparts paler. Has less bold eye-stripe and supercilium than Willow Warbler, and darker cheeks against which white under-eye crescent (half eye-ring) is prominent. Legs usually darkish. Call a short upslurred *hweet*, or downslurred *pyoo*. Song repeated steady *chiff-chaff-chiff-chaff*, with low growling notes audible at close range between song phrases. Found in woodland, scrub and parkland, larger gardens, wooded riversides. Usually feeds and sings high in trees, but nests low down. Common, widespread resident.

CETTI'S WARBLER *Cettia cetti* 13cm

A dark warbler with long, rounded tail. Upperparts warm, rich red-brown. Underparts grey-brown, barely paler than upperside, but with white throat. Faint darker mottling on undertail. Has slight pale supercilium, darker eye-stripe, dark half eye-ring. Wings very short, round-ended; tail has 'heavy' look but is often held cocked up. Calls loud, rich with fluty quality. Song short, loud, explosive series of very fluty notes. A very skulking bird, preferring thick cover with bushes and dense understorey, usually close to water. Creeps unobtrusively like rodent, though males in spring occasionally sing in open. A common, widespread resident.

LONG-TAILED TIT *Aegithalos caudatus* 14cm

Tiny short-billed, neckless tit-like bird, tail about 50% of total length. Whitish with blackish back, tail, wings and stripe above eye. Shoulders, flanks and belly washed rosy pink. Dark eye has orange eye-ring. Bill and legs dark. Juvenile lacks pink tints, and black head stripe extended to whole upper face; eye-ring red. Call a short purring *prrrrt*, also shorter *sst* notes. Social; at most times of year seen in family parties which follow one another from tree to tree. Found in woods, parks, gardens, scrubland and similar habitats; builds beautiful lichen-covered ball-shaped nest well hidden in bush. Common resident (not Sardinia).

▲ Adult male   ▲ Adult female

BLACKCAP *Sylvia atricapilla* 14cm

A sleek grey warbler. Upperparts unmarked mid grey-brown, underside a shade lighter. Male has black cap, female and juvenile reddish-brown cap (and slightly more brown-toned body plumage). White under-eye crescent, whitish undertail and throat. Cheeks grey rather than whitish as in Marsh and Willow Tits. Bill strong for warbler, legs grey. Call a hard *tac*, given repeatedly when alarmed. Song loud, very sweet and melodious short fluting phrases; also has softer, more mumbled and continuous subsong. Found in woodland, parks, gardens, scrub, hedgerows and riversides with trees; forages unobtrusively in foliage. Common, widespread resident.

GARDEN WARBLER *Sylvia borin* 14cm

Sturdy, very plain-looking warbler. Upperparts dull grey-brown with subtle pure grey wash on neck-sides. Underside paler; whitish undertail but strongly washed buff-brown on breast-sides and flanks. Face almost unmarked – very slight hint of eye-stripe and paler supercilium; dark eye prominent. Bill rather short and stout for warbler. Legs dark grey. Call a slightly throaty *chek*. Song recalls Blackcap's subsong; melodious but hurried, almost spluttering, in long phrases. Found in woodland, scrub, large parks, woodland edges; feeds on insects and berries, inconspicuous and best located by song. A summer visitor to north and north-east Italy only; passage migrant elsewhere.

SUBALPINE WARBLER *Sylvia cantillans* 12cm

Small, colourful, short-tailed warbler. Male upperparts dark blue-grey, shading to browner on wings. Throat and breast deep brick-red, gradually shading to pale pink on flanks, whitish on belly. Has prominent white stripe separating grey cheek from red throat; prominent red eye-ring. Legs pale pinkish. Female similar but much paler; juvenile rather plain brown but with dark-centred wing feathers. Call a dry *chak*, song a muddled series of twitters, trills and dry rattling phrases. Breeds in scrubland, woodland edges and other habitats with bushes. Fairly widespread summer visitor to most of Italy south of Tuscany; on Sardinia, passage migrant only.

MOLTONI'S WARBLER *Sylvia subalpina* 12cm

Very like Subalpine Warbler. Upperparts mid blue-grey, underparts soft pinkish-grey, becoming only slightly paler on belly. White line between grey cheek and pink throat is narrow, not very noticeable. Red eye-ring; pinkish legs. Female is washed-out version of male; juvenile similar to juvenile Subalpine Warbler. Call a dry, hard rattle. Song is similar to Subalpine's but distinctly faster and more frantic, often with hissing tone. Breeds from sea-level to low mountains in scrubland, woodland edges and other open habitats with bushes. Summer visitor, arriving slightly later than Subalpine Warbler; found in north-west Italy and on Sardinia; scarce passage migrant down mainland east coast.

▼ *Adult male*

▼ *Adult female*

▲ Adult male ▲ Adult female

SARDINIAN WARBLER *Sylvia melanocephala* 13cm

A slim, long-tailed, relatively large-headed warbler with bold manner. Male rather dark grey, paler on belly and undertail, with black head and white throat. Eye brown with prominent red eye-ring. Shows white tips to tail feathers when tail fanned. Female recalls dark male Common Whitethroat, with grey head and dark grey-brown body plumage, tinted pinkish on underparts, still with whitish throat, belly and undertail, and red eye-ring. Call a single *tschak* or fast, hard rattle; song a short, scratchy chatter. Breeds in warm open woodland and tall scrub, including in parks and gardens. A common resident, but rare and localised in far north.

LESSER WHITETHROAT *Sylvia curruca* 12cm

Small, rather short-tailed warbler. Sexes alike. Has grey crown with slightly darker cheeks, giving hint of face mask. Upperparts otherwise dull grey-brown. Underside pale with brown-washed flanks and bright white throat and undertail. Eyes dark with slight white 'spectacle' markings; legs dark grey. Call a soft, clicking *tet* or repeated churring scold. Song a simple short rattle, like Cirl Bunting; also a soft fast warbling. Found in scrub with scattered trees, woodland edges and similar well-vegetated open habitats, usually near or above tree-limit. Rather shy and unobtrusive, tends to sing from within cover. A fairly common summer visitor in Alps; passage migrant elsewhere.

▲ Adult male   ▲ Adult female

COMMON WHITETHROAT *Sylvia communis* 14cm

Slim warbler with relatively big head and long tail. Male has grey head with white eye-ring, grey-brown back and tail, wings bright rufous with dark feather centres (this is distinctive in all plumages). Underside pale, washed pinkish, throat bright white. Eyes light brown, legs pinkish. Female similar but browner on head. Juvenile like female, but eyes dark. Call a hard, nasal, scolding *djerr*. Song a fast, rather dry scratchy warble, often given in short, steeply rising song-flight. Found in bushy grassland, farmland with hedgerows, heaths, and other scrubby countryside of all kinds. Often conspicuous. A common and widespread summer visitor.

SPECTACLED WARBLER *Sylvia conspicillata* 12cm

Recalls petite, intensely coloured Common Whitethroat. Male has blue-grey-head, blackish around bill base, with bold white eye-ring. Back and tail grey-brown, wings rufous without obvious dark feather centres (so looks plainer) and shorter than Whitethroat's. Underside white, strongly washed pinkish, throat white. Female like miniature, small-billed female Whitethroat; wings plain bright rufous. Call a hard rattling *trrr*, song a rapid, high-pitched twitter, sometimes preceded by slower, purer notes. Breeds in scrubby open habitats, often in hilly upland countryside; tends to be shy and more difficult to observe than Whitethroat. A summer visitor to southern Italy, scarcer and more localised further north.

MARMORA'S WARBLER *Sylvia sarda* 13cm

Small, slender, very distinctive dark warbler with long tail and large head, crown often peaked and throat puffed out. Male uniform mid slate-grey, with dark throat but slightly paler undertail. Legs pinkish-orange, bill yellowish with dark tip, eye light brown with red eye-ring, lores blackish. Female very slightly browner grey, lacks dark lores so eye-ring less striking. Juvenile similar, tinted more brownish. Call a harsh, Stonechat-like *tchek*, song a rapid but sweet-toned warble. Found in dense scrubland on hillsides and down to coast level. Resident on Sardinia and some other islands, also rare winter visitor to far south of mainland Italy and Sicily.

DARTFORD WARBLER *Sylvia undata* 13cm

A dark warbler, more or less identical to Marmora's Warbler in shape and attitude but more colourful (though looks completely dark in poor light). Male is dark slate-grey on upperside, with dark rich purplish-red underside from throat to undertail; bright red eye-ring. Throat marked with fine white speckles. Legs yellowish. Female slightly less deeply-coloured version of male; juvenile rather dull earth-brown with slightly paler throat. Call a protracted *churr*; song a short rapid warble, mostly dry-toned but with a few fluted notes. Breeds in scrubby countryside; woodland edges, heaths, coastal bushes. Resident on mainland Italy, Sicily and Sardinia.

GOLDCREST *Regulus regulus* 9cm

Tiny, rounded, neckless bird with short tail. Plumage olive-green, paler below, with bold double white wing-bar. Top of crown yellow (orange-centred in male) with black edge. Eye prominent, circled with pale 'spectacle', dark line extending under eye from bill base; face otherwise plain. Legs dull brownish, bill dark, shortish and needle-like. Juvenile has plain grey-green crown. Call very high *tzee-tzee*, song a high-pitched rising and falling twittered phrase, ending in slightly rasping louder flourish. Found in woodland of all kinds, forages around thin twigs, often hovers. Fearless but very active. Breeds in Alps and Apennines, more widespread in winter elsewhere.

FIRECREST *Regulus ignicapilla* 9cm

Very like Goldcrest; same size and shape but a little more boldly patterned and colourful. Main difference is in face pattern; Firecrest has bold white supercilium and under-eye marking, with thin but clear black eye-stripe. Also has contrasting yellow-bronze patch on shoulder/neck-side, and upperparts are brighter green. Song and calls very like Goldcrest's but a little lower-pitched; song is simpler, essentially the same note repeated. Found in woodland but also more open scrubby countryside; more likely to forage at lower levels than Goldcrest, but not unusual for both species to be seen together in winter flocks. Fairly common and widespread resident.

SHORT-TOED TREECREEPER *Certhia brachydactyla* 13cm

Small bird that forages almost exclusively on tree trunks and branches. Upperparts mid-brown with paler streaks, has pale supercilium and cheek patch. 'Z'-shaped pattern of dark and light on folded flight feathers. Underside white, shading to brownish on rear flanks. Tail long and narrow, feather tips pointed. Bill long and down-curved. Legs pinkish, short but with strong toes for climbing and clinging. Call a ringing *tuit*; song a short, jerky phrase of similar-pitched notes. Climbs in spiral up tree trunks from base, probing bark cracks for food. Favours lowland woodlands, also parks and gardens. Common and widespread resident; not Sardinia.

TREECREEPER *Certhia familiaris* 13cm

Almost identical to Short-toed Treecreeper; best distinguished by voice, but is also a little whiter on underside, and 'Z' pattern in folded flight feathers is less clearly defined. Hind-claw a little longer, and bill a touch shorter. Call a very high, thin whistle, somewhat Goldcrest-like, with buzzy quality. Song also high and buzzy, a short phrase falling in pitch and finishing with trill. Behaviour like Short-toed Treecreeper, but is less widespread, preferring upland mixed or pine forests, while Short-toed more likely in low-lying deciduous woodland. A common resident in Alps, scarcer and more localised in Apennines and south Italy; absent from Sicily and Sardinia.

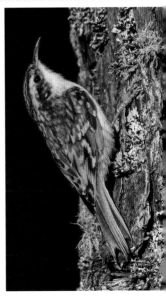

NUTHATCH *Sitta europaea* 13cm

A dapper, agile, tree-climbing bird with large head, long strong bill and short tail. Upperparts from crown to tail mid blue-grey. Has long black eye-stripe, with white cheeks below, shading gradually to warm orange-buff. In male, colour darkens to almost brick-red on undertail, with contrasting white spots; remains paler in female. Legs pinkish, very sturdy with strongly curved claws. Call a loud, ringing *tuit* or *vit*; song made up of similar notes repeated. Woodland bird, climbs on tree trunks (including downwards head-first), takes insects, also wedges nuts in bark cracks and hammers them open. Common resident; local in Sicily and absent in Sardinia.

WALLCREEPER *Tichodroma muraria* 16cm

Very striking mountain bird; shaped like a treecreeper but with longer, thinner bill. Blue-grey body plumage, becoming white on throat and breast. Wings have extensive deep pink-red patches. Breeding-plumaged male acquires black lower face and throat. Legs and bill black. In flight shows white spots near wingtips, white tail-corners, and strikingly round, butterfly-like wing-shape. Not very vocal; song a series of soft rising and falling whistles. Climbs on steep rock faces; probes cracks for prey. Breeds in mountains but may move to lower ground (and visit quarries, buildings) in winter. Resident in Alps and Apennines; more widespread in winter, even on sea-cliffs.

WREN *Troglodytes troglodytes* 10cm

Very small, rounded, short-tailed bird with longish, slightly down-curved bill. Plumage brown, a shade paler and greyer on underparts, marked all over with fine darker barring. Dark eye-stripe, pale supercilium. Legs pinkish, rather long, feet strong. Posture often hunched forwards but nearly always holds tail cocked upright over back. Call a hard, dry rattle or single *clak* note; song very loud series of fast, hard rattling trills. Often forages on ground, clambering mouse-like through dense vegetation, but will sing from raised, conspicuous perch. Prefers habitats with good ground cover; woodlands, gardens, hedgerows, scrubland. A very common, widespread resident.

STARLING *Sturnus vulgaris* 21cm

Dark, glossy bird with short tail, strong pointed bill, upright stance and bustling walk. In breeding season, uniform blackish glossed green and violet, a few paler spots. Bill yellow (pale bluish-grey at base in male). In winter similar but with numerous whitish spots; bill darker. Juvenile uniform light brown with dark lores and pale throat; gradually develops spotted winter plumage. Legs pinkish. Very vocal. Various harsh calls; song includes metallic buzzes, high whistles, and much mimicry. Open habitats; farmland, parks, towns; mainly forages on ground and usually in flocks. Common resident in northern and central Italy, scarce in south; more widespread and locally abundant in winter.

SPOTLESS STARLING *Sturnus unicolor* 21cm

Very like Starling but less glossy, with sheen toned purple without green tints. Entirely unspotted in breeding plumage. In winter plumage has fine paler spots but much less conspicuously spotty than Starling. Legs lighter, brighter pink than Starling's. Juvenile darker than juvenile Starling, with entirely dark upper face. Voice similar to Starling's but with sharper, clearer tone to some notes. Behaviour similar to Starling's; mainly forages on ground, walking briskly and pausing to probe soil with bill. Gregarious. Usually breeds and forages close to human habitation; farmland, parks and similar open ground. Resident on Sicily and Sardinia only.

DIPPER *Cinclus cinclus* 19cm

Unique riverine songbird; stout and short-tailed, recalling oversized Wren in shape. Adult dark brown, tinted russet on head and belly, hint of paler scaling on upperparts. Throat and breast white with crisp edge. Juvenile very grey with prominent paler scaling, throat white but breast and belly barred grey. Flight call a sharp *tzit*; song a varied, slow-paced phrase of rather tuneless notes. Found alongside fast-flowing rivers and streams with rocks to use as perches, from where it plunges into water and finds prey on river bed. Flies fast and low between foraging areas; also floats downstream with current. Uncommon, widespread resident.

SPOTTED FLYCATCHER *Muscicapa striata* 14cm

Sleek, plain flycatcher with slim body, large head, short legs and long wings. Adult dull grey-brown on upperparts, with crown, breast and flanks whitish marked with brown streaks; belly and undertail unmarked whitish. Juvenile similar but has prominent pale spotting on back and wings. Legs dark. Call a short *see*, song a short, rather slow phrase of scratchy notes. Perches in very upright stance before flying out to catch a fly, often returning to same perch. Found in woodland with sunny clearings, parks and gardens. Nests in tree holes or crevices in walls. A fairly common, widespread summer visitor.

ROBIN *Erithacus rubecula* 13cm

A round-bodied, smallish chat. Adult has brown upperparts and orange-red face and breast, variably broad greyish line separating red from brown on cheeks and breast-sides. May show narrow paler wing-bar. Belly whitish, cleanly separated from red breast, brown tinge on flanks. Eye prominent, large and dark. Legs dark. Juvenile uniform warm mid-brown with extensive creamy spotting. Call a sharp *tic*; song sweet, melancholic twitters and trills, including slow phrases. Often perches with tail raised, wings drooping. Usually forages on the ground, taking invertebrates; also feeds on berries. Found in all kinds of habitats with trees and some ground cover. Common resident, more widespread in winter.

NIGHTINGALE *Luscinia megarhynchos* 16cm

Fairly large chat, recalling an all-brown, long-tailed Robin. Plumage rather uniform warm mid-brown, with greyish wash on neck-sides, and slightly paler breast shading to whitish belly. Eye dark with subtle paler eye-ring, legs pinkish. Tail has strong rufous tint, striking in flight. Frequently perches with tail raised and wings drooping. Has various soft, nondescript calls. Song exceptional; powerfully throbbing, fluting phrases alternating with slow, high single-note whistles, given by day and through night. Very skulking, reluctant to leave cover. Found in woodland with dense, tangled undergrowth, also scrubby woodland edges and large gardens. Common, widespread summer visitor.

PIED FLYCATCHER *Ficedula hypoleuca* 13cm

A compact, relatively rounded and short-tailed flycatcher. Male usually has black upperparts with white forehead patch and large white wing patch, with adjoining very small extra wing-bar. Underparts from throat to undertail pure white. Female has similar pattern but black areas replaced with grey-brown; lacks forehead patch and has less white in wing than male. Some males are more brownish-black and close to female in tone. Legs black. Call a sharp *tik*; song a loud, rather unmelodic pulsing trill with slight changes in pitch. Prefers open, sunny oak woodland but will use other kinds of wooded habitats on migration. A widespread passage migrant in Italy.

▼ *Adult male*   ▼ *Adult female*

COLLARED FLYCATCHER *Ficedula albicollis* 13cm

Very like Pied Flycatcher but with more extensive white. Male has very large white forehead patch, and complete white collar. Rump white, with diffuse edges. White wing patch large, with adjoining broad white wing-bar. Female very like female Pied Flycatcher; white wing-bar broader. Call a thin whistle. Song a slow sequence of slightly rasping whistles, shifting considerably in pitch. Breeds in open sunny deciduous woodlands, parks, gardens and similar habitats, nesting in tree holes (often old woodpecker nests) and feeding on insects caught in flight. Rather patchily distributed summer visitor to central and south mainland Italy; passage migrant elsewhere.

COMMON REDSTART *Phoenicurus phoenicurus* 14cm

Slender chat with long wings. Male colourful (especially in spring), with blue-grey crown, back and wings, white flash on forehead, black face and throat, orange-red breast and belly. Legs blackish. Female and juvenile rather plain warm brown with pale-circled dark eyes, and reddish wash to breast and flanks. In all plumages has red rump and red, dark-centred tail which it frequently shivers. Call *tick-tick* and soft *tuit*; song a pleasant descending twittered phrase, somewhat like Chaffinch but more varied and lacking final flourish. Found in deciduous woodland, parks and large gardens. A fairly widespread summer visitor, and widespread passage migrant.

▼ *Adult male*   ▼ *Adult female*

▲ Adult male

▲ Adult female

BLACK REDSTART *Phoenicurus ochruros* **14cm**

In shape and habits very like Common Redstart. Male has rather uniform sooty blackish plumage, darkest on face and breast, fading to whitish on belly, and often has paler forehead. Variably prominent white panel in wing. Female, juvenile and some younger males are uniform dull grey-brown, slightly paler on belly. Tail and rump red in all plumages. Call a short whistle, song a simple twitter interspersed with curious quiet grinding noises. Prefers open, rugged countryside with bare ground, and also urban environments; nests in crevice in rock or building. A fairly widespread resident, with migrants from further north arriving in winter.

ROCK THRUSH *Monticola saxatilis* **19cm**

Large, stocky, short-tailed and long-winged thrush-like chat. Male colourful, with blue-grey head and upper back, deep brick-red breast and belly, dark wings, white lower back and red, dark-centred tail. Female uniform brown, a shade lighter and redder on the underside, with pale scaling on upperparts and dark barring on underparts; reddish tail. Warmer-toned than female Blue Rock Thrush. Legs dark. Call a hard *chat* or softer *whst*; song quiet, melodious with melancholy tone; often given in undulating, bat-like display flight. Mainly found in montane areas above 1,500 metres, with steep cliff faces and areas of grassland. A localised summer visitor and passage migrant.

▼ Adult male

▼ Adult female

▲ Adult male   ▲ Adult female

BLUE ROCK THRUSH *Monticola solitarius* 22cm

Larger and longer-tailed than Rock Thrush, with distinctly longer bill. Male deep dark blue with darker wings and tail; looks completely black in all but good light. Female dark brown, uniform on upperside but paler below with strong dark barring; no rufous tones. Legs dark. Has a two-note call and a single low-pitched *chek*; song like Rock Thrush's but louder, with quavering notes. A bird of rocky habitats, usually at lower altitudes than Rock Thrush and found down to sea-level, also in towns (but still tends to be shy and flighty, though chooses conspicuous perches). Fairly common, widespread resident.

WHINCHAT *Saxicola rubetra* 13cm

A small, rotund but long-winged chat, distinguished in all plumages by the long, broad, pale or white supercilium and white tail base. Male is boldy marked with blackish crown and cheeks, white supercilium and cheek-sides, orange breast shading to white belly, and sandy-brown upperparts with strong dark streaks; small white wing patch. Female similar but head markings duller, more uniform. Calls are soft clicks and whistles, song a short, varied phrase with harsh and more tuneful notes; will sing at night. Chooses prominent perches. Prefers remote, damp open countryside; wet scrubby meadows, moorland, forest edges. A rather localised summer visitor and widespread passage migrant.

▼ Adult male breeding   ▼ Adult female

▲ Adult male breeding   ▲ Adult female

STONECHAT *Saxicola rubicola* 12cm

A little stouter and shorter-winged than Whinchat. Male has black head and blackish upperparts with dark cheeks, prominent white neck-sides, and orange underside down to belly. Rump pale; sometimes white, sometimes buff with dark streaks. Narrow white shoulder patch. Female similar but paler, head brown, lacks white neck patches. Call a high note followed by stone-tapping sounds (*weet tak-tak*), song a brief, Dunnock-like twitter. Perches in full view atop bush or post, dropping to ground to catch insects. Found in open but well-vegetated habitats in lowlands and uplands; heaths, alpine meadows, waste ground. A common and widespread resident.

NORTHERN WHEATEAR *Oenanthe oenanthe* 15cm

Rather large, slim chat with upright posture and long wings. Male light blue-grey on crown and back, with black wings and eye-mask, white supercilium. Underside pale with orange-pink flush on breast, becoming white on lower belly. Female paler and browner; mask reduced to brownish eye-stripe. Juvenile dull grey with scaly markings, becoming female-like but very orange-toned after first moult. In all plumages shows white rump, and white tail with black centre and black band at tip. Typical chat-like whistle and *chak* calls, song a rapid dry chirruping. Prefers open rocky habitats with short or sparse vegetation. Fairly widespread summer visitor.

▼ Adult male breeding   ▼ Adult female breeding

EASTERN BLACK-EARED WHEATEAR
Oenanthe melanoleuca **14cm**

Smaller and rounder than Wheatear. Male whitish with black face and wings (a few have pale throat); crown, back and breast-sides have sandy tint. Female rather uniform earth-brown with slightly paler underside, no strong face markings. Male in fresh autumn plumage much browner than spring male. In all plumages shows white rump and tail-sides; centre, tip and lower sides of tail black. Calls like Northern Wheatear's; also a hissing note. Song a fast, dry twittering, similar to Common Whitethroat, and may include mimicry. Found in open, arid countryside with some bushes, riversides, sometimes around villages. A summer visitor to mainly south Italy; very localised further north.

▷ *From top: adult male breeding, adult female breeding, male pale throat morph*

MISTLE THRUSH *Turdus viscivorus* **28cm**

The largest thrush; long-tailed, pot-bellied and small-headed. Upperside light sandy brown with conspicuous pale edges to wing feathers. Underside pale with dense round spots over entire breast and belly. In flight shows white inner part of underwing and pale tail corners. Call a hard dry rattle, very loud when mobbing predators; song a loud, powerful fluting but rather simple phrase. Feeds on the ground, hopping strongly and pulling worms from soil. Found in mainly open habitats but with some trees for nesting; parks, gardens, woodland edges, mountainsides. Fairly common and widespread resident in mountains, scarcer in north and east.

SONG THRUSH   *Turdus philomelos*   21cm

Smaller than Mistle Thrush with different proportions. Upperside uniform warm mid-brown. Underside whitish with strong yellowy wash to breast-sides. Spots are teardrop-shaped and become small and sparse on centre of belly. In flight shows all-brown, rather short tail, and yellowish-orange inner part to underwing. Call a rather soft *tic*. Song comprises short, fluting phrases, each repeated once or a few times before next phrase begins. Feeds on ground and in bushes, taking invertebrates and berries, and also strikes snails against stones ('thrush anvils') to break them. Resident in central mainland Italy from north to south, winter visitor and passage migrant elsewhere.

REDWING   *Turdus iliacus*   21cm

(Near Threatened) A little shorter-tailed than Song Thrush. Upperside dark brown with pale edges to wing feathers. Has prominent white supercilium and cheek-sides, dark eye-stripe. Spots on breast coalesce into streaks on flanks. Rear flanks and inner part of underwing bright rusty-red. Call a high, grating whistle, *zeeeh*, noticeable at night as flocks migrate overhead. Song (which may be heard close to spring migration time) a very varied sequence of whistled, fluty and squeaky notes. Gregarious in winter and often roams in flocks with other thrushes, visiting stands of berry-bearing trees and bushes, and foraging on bare fields. A widespread but scarce winter visitor.

▲ Adult male

▲ Adult female

BLACKBIRD *Turdus merula* 26cm

Sleek, dark, long-tailed thrush. Male entirely black without noticeable gloss; legs dark, bill and eye-ring yellow. Female dark brown with variable paler throat and vague speckling on breast and belly; bill orange or blackish. Juvenile lighter warm brown with yellowish spotting; flight feathers black in male juveniles, browner in females. Call a liquid *chuck* or more agitated *quick-quick-quick*. Song a beautiful strong fluting at varied but generally quite slow pace. Hops on ground, listening for prey; also takes berries and windfall fruit. Found in woodland, parks, gardens and other habitats with some bushes or trees and some open ground. Common, widespread resident.

FIELDFARE *Turdus pilaris* 25cm

Rather colourful, large thrush. Head, lower back and rump light grey, upper back and shoulders dark red-brown, tail black, underside white with strong orange wash on breast, marked with black streaks that become chevrons on flanks; central belly and inner part of underwing strikingly white. Has blackish lores and white supercilium. Call a loud clucking chuckle *chek-chek*. Song a rather simple chatter. As with Redwing, forms roving winter flocks which seek berry-bushes, orchards, ploughed fields and other foraging grounds, so may be found in many kinds of open countryside. A widespread winter visitor, scarcer in the south.

GLOSSARY

Bare parts The unfeathered parts of a bird – legs, bill and sometimes parts of the face.

Bib A patch of colour covering the throat and upper breast.

Breast-band A stripe of colour across the breast.

Call A simple sound made by a bird, for contact or to warn of danger.

Crest A tuft of feathers on top of a bird's head.

Drumming (in woodpeckers) Repeatedly striking a resonant tree branch or trunk with the bill; equivalent to song.

Ear-tufts Tufts of feathers on either side of the top of a bird's head.

Eye-mask A patch of contrasting colour over the eye and upper cheek.

Eye-ring A circle of coloured feathers or bare skin around the eye.

Eye-stripe A line (usually dark) of colour running in front of and behind the eye.

Facial disc The face of an owl, outlined by a ruff of short, stiff feathers.

Feral Describes wild-living birds that are descended from captive stock.

Fringes The edges of feathers, often contrastingly coloured to give a scaly appearance.

Invertebrate Animals without a backbone – insects, spiders, snails etc.

Iridescent Having a brightly coloured sheen in certain lights.

Leading edge (of wing) The front edge of the opened wing as the bird is flying.

Lores Area between the base of the bill and the eye.

Moustachial stripe A (usually dark) stripe running down the cheek.

Passage migrant A bird that occurs in a certain area only during its migratory journey – passing through.

Passerine Songbird or 'perching bird'.

Primaries The outermost flight feathers, or 'hand' of the wing.

Resident A bird that is present in a certain area all year round.

Scrub Any habitat with plenty of bushes but few or no trees.

Secondaries The inner flight feathers, or 'arm' of the wing.

Song Sound made by a bird (usually male) to advertise its territory; more complex than calls.

Song-flight A particular type of flight (usually rising then falling) performed as the bird sings.

Subsong Variation of typical song, usually quieter.

Supercilium A line of colour (usually pale) above the eye, in an 'eyebrow' position.

Tail-band A stripe of colour across the tail, most often the tail-tip.

Trailing edge (of wing) The rear edge of the opened wing as a bird flies.

Upperparts The top side of a bird – usually crown, neck, back, upperside of wings, rump and upperside of tail.

Underparts The bottom side of a bird – usually throat, breast, belly, flanks, underside of wings, and underside of tail.

Wattle A conspicuous fleshy growth of coloured skin on a bird's face.

Wing-bar A stripe of contrasting colour on the wing, usually visible when wing is folded as well as spread.

FURTHER READING

The following books should be of interest to those wishing to learn more about the birds, birdwatching and other wildlife of Italy:

Jepson, Tim, *Wild Italy: A Traveller's Guide*, Sheldrake Press, London, 2005. A detailed site guide for places to enjoy wildlife-watching, hiking and other outdoor activities in Italy.

Lega Italiana Protezione Uccelli, *Where to Watch Birds in Italy*, Christopher Helm, London, 1994. A guide to the best birdwatching sites in Italy.

Price, Gillian. *Walking in Sicily*, Cicerone Guides, Kendal, 2014. One of several walking guides for Italy published by Cicerone Press, giving tried-and-tested walks of varied length and difficulty through beautiful wild scenery.

Svensson, Lars, *Collins Bird Guide*, Collins, London, 2009. Detailed and comprehensive identification guide to birds of Britain and Europe, including most species recorded in Italy to date.

PHOTO CREDITS

All the photographs in this book were taken by Daniele Occhiato, with the exception of the following: Carlos Naza Bocos: 19B, 58T, 97T, 125T; Luca Borra: 65BL; Richard Brooks/FLPA: 131T; Lorenzo Ercoli: 77TL, 77TR, 79BL; Saverio Gatto: 67T, 125B; Paul Hurlimann: 98BR; Lorenzo Magnolfi: 105T; Marko Matesic, BIA/Minden Pictures/FLPA: 17T; Michele Mendi: 20B, 63B, 66B, 68B, 72B, 84TR, 86T, 97BL; Stefano Turri: 60T, 98BL.

ACKNOWLEDGEMENTS

Marianne Taylor would like to thank Jim Martin, Jane Lawes and Jenny Campbell at Bloomsbury for guiding this book from conception to completion. She would also like to thank Daniele Occhiato for his superb photographs and invaluable feedback on the text, and Susan McIntyre, Tim Harris and Frances Cooper for their work on the layout, editing and proofreading respectively.

LIST OF ENGLISH AND ITALIAN NAMES

English – Italian

Greylag Goose – *Oca selvatica*
Red-breasted Merganser – *Smergo minore*
Shelduck – *Volpoca*
Pochard – *Moriglione*
Ferruginous Duck – *Moretta tabaccata*
Tufted Duck – *Moretta*
Garganey – *Marzaiola*
Shoveler – *Mestolone*
Gadwall – *Canapiglia*
Wigeon – *Fischione*
Mallard – *Germano reale*
Pintail – *Codone*
Eurasian Teal – *Alzavola*
Common Quail – *Quaglia*
Rock Partridge – *Coturnice*
Barbary Partridge – *Pernice sarda*
Red-legged Partridge – *Pernice rossa*
Common Pheasant – *Fagiano*
Hazel Grouse – *Francolino di monte*
Ptarmigan – *Pernice bianca*
Capercaillie – *Gallo cedrone*
Black Grouse – *Fagiano di monte*
Greater Flamingo – *Fenicottero*

English – Italian

Little Grebe – *Tuffetto*
Great Crested Grebe – *Svasso maggiore*
Black-necked Grebe – *Svasso piccolo*
Woodpigeon – *Colombaccio*
Turtle Dove – *Tortora*
Collared Dove – *Tortora dal collare*
European Nightjar – *Succiacapre*
Alpine Swift – *Rondone maggiore*
Pallid Swift – *Rondone pallido*
Common Swift – *Rondone*
Common Cuckoo – *Cuculo*
Water Rail – *Porciglione*
Spotted Crake – *Voltolino*
Little Crake – *Schiribilla*
Moorhen – *Gallinella d'acqua*
Coot – *Folaga*
Common Crane – *Gru*
Red-throated Diver – *Strolaga minore*
Black-throated Diver – *Strolaga mezzana*
Scopoli's Shearwater – *Berta maggiore*
Yelkouan Shearwater – *Berta minore mediterranea*
White Stork – *Cicogna bianca*
Bittern – *Tarabuso*

English – Italian

Little Bittern – *Tarabusino*
Night Heron – *Nitticora*
Squacco Heron – *Sgarza ciuffetto*
Cattle Egret – *Airone guardabuoi*
Grey Heron – *Airone cenerino*
Purple Heron – *Airone rosso*
Great Egret – *Airone bianco maggiore*
Little Egret – *Garzetta*
African Sacred Ibis – *Ibis sacro*
Eurasian Spoonbill – *Spatola*
Glossy Ibis – *Mignattaio*
Northern Gannet – *Sula*
Shag – *Marangone dal ciuffo*
Cormorant – *Cormorano*
Stone-curlew – *Occhione*
Oystercatcher – *Beccaccia di mare*
Avocet – *Avocetta*
Black-winged Stilt – *Cavaliere d'Italia*
Grey Plover – *Pivieressa*
Golden Plover – *Piviere dorato*
Ringed Plover – *Corriere grosso*
Little Ringed Plover – *Corriere piccolo*
Kentish Plover – *Fratino*
Lapwing – *Pavoncella*
Whimbrel – *Chiurlo piccolo*
Curlew – *Chiurlo maggiore*
Bar-tailed Godwit – *Pittima minore*
Black-tailed Godwit – *Pittima reale*
Turnstone – *Voltapietre*
Ruff – *Combattente*
Curlew Sandpiper – *Piovanello comune*
Temminck's Stint – *Gambecchio nano*
Sanderling – *Piovanello tridattilo*
Dunlin – *Piovanello pancianera*
Little Stint – *Gambecchio*
Woodcock – *Beccaccia*
Common Snipe – *Beccaccino*
Common Sandpiper – *Piro piro piccolo*
Green Sandpiper – *Piro piro culbianco*
Spotted Redshank – *Totano moro*
Greenshank – *Pantana*
Common Redshank – *Pettegola*
Wood Sandpiper – *Piro piro boschereccio*
Collared Pratincole – *Pernice di mare*
Slender-billed Gull – *Gabbiano roseo*
Black-headed Gull – *Gabbiano comune*
Mediterranean Gull – *Gabbiano corallino*
Audouin's Gull – *Gabbiano corso*
Lesser Black-backed Gull – *Zafferano*
Yellow-legged Gull – *Gabbiano reale*
Little Tern – *Fraticello*
Gull-billed Tern – *Sterna zampenere*
Whiskered Tern – *Mignattino piombato*
White-winged Black Tern – *Mignattino alibianche*

English – Italian

Black Tern – *Mignattino*
Common Tern – *Sterna comune*
Sandwich Tern – *Beccapesci*
Osprey – *Falco pescatore*
European Honey-buzzard – *Falco pecchiaiolo*
Short-toed Eagle – *Biancone*
Griffon Vulture – *Grifone*
Golden Eagle – *Aquila reale*
Booted Eagle – *Aquila minore*
Marsh Harrier – *Falco di palude*
Hen Harrier – *Albanella reale*
Montagu's Harrier – *Albanella minore*
Sparrowhawk – *Sparviero*
Goshawk – *Astore*
Red Kite – *Nibbio reale*
Black Kite – *Nibbio bruno*
Common Buzzard – *Poiana*
Barn Owl – *Barbagianni*
Little Owl – *Civetta*
Scops Owl – *Assiolo*
Long-eared Owl – *Gufo comune*
Tawny Owl – *Allocco*
Hoopoe – *Upupa*
Wryneck – *Torcicollo*
Green Woodpecker – *Picchio verde*
Black Woodpecker – *Picchio nero*
Lesser Spotted Woodpecker – *Picchio rosso minore*
Great Spotted Woodpecker – *Picchio rosso maggiore*
European Bee-eater – *Gruccione*
Roller – *Ghiandaia marina*
Kingfisher – *Martin pescatore*
Lesser Kestrel – *Grillaio*
Common Kestrel – *Gheppio*
Red-footed Falcon – *Falco cuculo*
Eleonora's Falcon – *Falco della regina*
Hobby – *Lodolaio*
Lanner Falcon – *Lanario*
Peregrine Falcon – *Falco pellegrino*
Rose-ringed Parakeet – *Parrocchetto dal collare*
Golden Oriole – *Rigogolo*
Red-backed Shrike – *Averla piccola*
Lesser Grey Shrike – *Averla cenerina*
Woodchat Shrike – *Averla capirossa*
Great Grey Shrike – *Averla maggiore*
Chough – *Gracchio corallino*
Alpine Chough – *Gracchio alpino*
Jay – *Ghiandaia*
Magpie – *Gazza*
Nutcracker – *Nocciolaia*
Jackdaw – *Taccola*
Rook – *Corvo*

English – Italian

Raven – *Corvo imperiale*
Carrion Crow – *Cornacchia nera*
Hooded Crow – *Cornacchia grigia*
Alpine Accentor – *Sordone*
Dunnock – *Passera scopaiola*
House Sparrow – *Passera oltremontana*
Italian Sparrow – *Passera d'Italia*
Spanish Sparrow – *Passera sarda*
Tree Sparrow – *Passera mattugia*
White-winged Snowfinch – *Fringuello alpino*
Tree Pipit – *Prispolone*
Meadow Pipit – *Pispola*
Water Pipit – *Spioncello*
Tawny Pipit – *Calandro*
Yellow Wagtail – *Cutrettola*
Grey Wagtail – *Ballerina gialla*
White Wagtail – *Ballerina bianca*
Chaffinch – *Fringuello*
Brambling – *Peppola*
Hawfinch – *Frosone*
Bullfinch – *Ciuffolotto*
Greenfinch – *Verdone*
Linnet – *Fanello*
Common Redpoll – *Organetto*
Common Crossbill – *Crociere*
Goldfinch – *Cardellino*
Corsican Finch / Citril Finch – *Venturone corso / Venturone alpino*
Serin – *Verzellino*
Siskin – *Lucherino*
Black-headed Bunting – *Zigolo capinero*
Corn Bunting – *Strillozzo*
Rock Bunting – *Zigolo muciatto*
Ortolan Bunting – *Ortolano*
Cirl Bunting – *Zigolo nero*
Yellowhammer – *Zigolo giallo*
Reed Bunting – *Migliarino di palude*
Coal Tit – *Cincia mora*
Crested Tit – *Cincia dal ciuffo*
Willow Tit – *Cincia bigia alpestre*
Marsh Tit – *Cincia bigia*
Blue Tit – *Cinciarella*
Great Tit – *Cinciallegra*
Penduline Tit – *Pendolino*
Calandra Lark – *Calandra*
Short-toed Lark – *Calandrella*
Woodlark – *Tottavilla*
Skylark – *Allodola*
Crested Lark – *Cappellaccia*
Bearded Tit – *Basettino*
Zitting Cisticola – *Beccamoschino*
Savi's Warbler – *Salciaiola*
Melodious Warbler – *Canapino*
Moustached Warbler – *Forapaglie castagnolo*

English – Italian

Sedge Warbler – *Forapaglie*
Marsh Warbler – *Cannaiola verdognola*
Reed Warbler – *Cannaiola*
Great Reed Warbler – *Cannareccione*
House Martin – *Balestruccio*
Barn Swallow – *Rondine*
Crag Martin – *Rondine montana*
Sand Martin – *Topino*
Western Bonelli's Warbler – *Luì bianco*
Wood Warbler – *Luì verde*
Willow Warbler – *Luì grosso*
Chiffchaff – *Luì piccolo*
Cetti's Warbler – *Usignolo di fiume*
Long-tailed Tit – *Codibugnolo*
Blackcap – *Capinera*
Garden Warbler – *Beccafico*
Eastern Subalpine Warbler – *Sterpazzolina comune*
Moltoni's Warbler – *Sterpazzolina di Moltoni*
Sardinian Warbler – *Occhiocotto*
Lesser Whitethroat – *Bigiarella*
Common Whitethroat – *Sterpazzola*
Spectacled Warbler – *Sterpazzola di Sardegna*
Marmora's Warbler – *Magnanina sarda*
Dartford Warbler – *Magnanina*
Goldcrest – *Regolo*
Firecrest – *Fiorrancino*
Short-toed Treecreeper – *Rampichino*
Treecreeper – *Rampichino alpestre*
Nuthatch – *Picchio muratore*
Wallcreeper – *Picchio muraiolo*
Wren – *Scricciolo*
Starling – *Storno*
Spotless Starling – *Storno nero*
Dipper – *Merlo acquaiolo*
Spotted Flycatcher – *Pigliamosche*
Robin – *Pettirosso*
Nightingale – *Usignolo*
Pied Flycatcher – *Balia nera*
Collared Flycatcher – *Balia dal collare*
Common Redstart – *Codirosso*
Black Redstart – *Codirosso spazzacamino*
Rock Thrush – *Codirossone*
Blue Rock Thrush – *Passero solitario*
Whinchat – *Stiaccino*
Stonechat – *Saltimpalo*
Northern Wheatear – *Culbianco*
Eastern Black-eared Wheatear – *Monachella orientale*
Mistle Thrush – *Tordela*
Song Thrush – *Tordo bottaccio*
Redwing – *Tordo sassello*
Blackbird – *Merlo*
Fieldfare – *Cesena*

INDEX

142